Nick de Voil has written a superb intro͏~ ͏~experience landscape. An essential read f͏~ ͏~ ͏~ ͏~ ͏~ ͏~ to create user-centred products or services that solve real problems for humans, regardless of their job title.

Chris Burns, *Product Manager, MoteHQ*

This book gives all the steps needed to ensure products and services are useful, usable and actually used. Nick de Voil brings his considerable experience to identify what's both similar and different between user experience and other traditional practices. All this results in a must-read and approachable book.

Kate Tarling, *Director of Digital, Design and Research, Services Work*

User Experience Foundations offers a comprehensive and standard-setting syllabus to UX. Its clear and concise explanations of key concepts, step-by-step method guides and practical hands-on tips will help anyone wanting to master the craft of real-world user experience.

John Knight, *Global Service Design Strategy Lead, Avanade*

This book is a good reference for new UX practitioners or anyone who wants to deepen their understanding of user experience. UX is a continuously growing field. This book provides a breadth of information on the subject with practical tips. You'll get an excellent foundation of knowledge from it.

Chui Chui Tan, *Director and Founder, Beyō Global*

User Experience Foundations is nicely written, easy to digest and covers the fundamentals of UX. Nick has covered all bases, from user testing techniques to where UX fits in with other disciplines. A must read for anybody considering a role in UX or simply looking to gain knowledge in this area.

Adrian Robinson, *Lead Agile Business Analyst,*
CDL (Cheshire Datasystems Limited)

This excellent primer blends theory and practice from a number of sources to provide a practical and accessible overview. Crucial reading!

Adrian Reed, *Principal Consultant, Blackmetric*

Nick de Voil has unlocked the foundations of the user experience (UX) discipline to simply describe what UX professionals ought to do, why they do it and why it works. It challenges what UX is in the construct of user-centred design principles that act as guideposts to optimise user experience.

Milvio DiBartolomeo, *ICT Portfolio, Programme and Project Professional*

Nick de Voil has written an invaluable guide on how UX supports digital product development and how to design experiences which meet people's needs. This book is a good reference for those starting their career in UX as well as product owners, business analysts and digital marketeers.

Nichola Musgrove, *Senior User Experience Designer, Ordnance Survey*

Nick de Voil is spot on with the details needed to understand the field of human centred design. He clearly explains how user research is integral to good design. This is a great starting point for anyone getting to grips with user experience work.

Franny Gant, *Senior User Researcher, Care Quality Commission*

If you're considering a User Experience role, there is a lot to learn - guiding principles, context of use, usability evaluation. This book gives a 360-degree view of this fascinating role and how it fits the big picture of a whole software development lifecycle!

Ahmed Tealeb, *Senior Software Development Engineer in Test,*
Ministry of Interior, State of Qatar

I was so excited to read this book as we often struggle with stakeholders who don't always understand the importance of UX when designing new products and services. This book really hits the nail on the head and is brilliant for anyone wanting to get their head around user experience design and research and its importance.

Katie Derham, *Innovation Manager, Allen and Overy LLP*

It seems everyone talks about UX, yet it is often misunderstood. Fortunately, there is a recognised standard at the core of UX and Human Centred Design which Nick de Voil uses as a framework in this clear overview of the HCD process and UX activities. I highly recommended this book as a pragmatic, easy to read introduction to this important and fascinating field.

Chris Rourke, *Founder and CEO, User Vision*

A business analyst often needs to be a jack of all trades with a foundation-level understanding of many subject areas and a comprehensive toolbox of techniques to draw from. This book succeeds in adding a solid understanding of the professional discipline of UX backed up by a comprehensive set of techniques and recommended practices.

Mark Ainsworth, *Business Analyst, Promising ICT Limited*

As UX has matured over the last ten years, there is a higher expectation to describe the rationale behind every pixel on the screen. This book helps to tell that vital story of WHY with context and tactics to handle any design situation. Nick de Voil has done a great job condensing the vast subject of UX into this book for those new to the field of UX, current practitioners, experts and those with a vested interest.

Paul Wilshaw, *Head of UX and UI, Blue Prism Ltd*

This book provides a good introduction to UX and user-centred design to accompany and prepare for BCS foundation level UX certification. In addition, Nick de Voil shares valuable advice to aid practical application. I particularly enjoyed the easily accessible chapter on 'illustrating the context of use' and the advice on designing simplified useful systems.

Michael Greenhalgh, *Director, Business Engagement and Analysis, British Council*

User experience encompasses many still-emerging practices, making teaching and learning interesting and challenging all at once. This book does well to provide a comprehensive overview of its fundamentals.

Boon Yew Chew, *Principal Designer, Elsevier and Local Leader, IxDA London*

An informative introduction to UX which will enable the reader to navigate confidently. The book dispels commonly misunderstood terms and provides a practical framework to deliver UX. A must read for the modern digital business analysts.

Rizwana Qureshi, *Business Analysis Capability Lead, Hitachi Vantara*

This book distils the knowledge of several books and international standards into an easy-to-read form that is accessible for beginners and experts alike. Its comprehensive list of references and engaging exercises make it an invaluable learning resource. I recommend it to everyone who wishes to gain an understanding of user experience.

Tamer El-Tonsy, *HCM Solutions Architect and Business Analyst, Tatonsy Consulting*

I recommend all business analysts read the book to add a new dimension to their work, maximize their results and improve communication with the user experiences experts.

Mohamed Zahran, *Lead Business Analyst, e-finance and IIBA Egypt Chapter President*

A concise and very well-crafted piece of knowledge about UX, Usability and UCD/HCD in general. I wish I had it for my students when I was teaching UX myself. During my career both as a leader of the company and as a consultant in HCD field I found it particularly important to have a common language with all the stakeholders. Among other good things this book does that one particularly well!

Yuri Vedenin, *Founder and President, UXPressia*

USER EXPERIENCE FOUNDATIONS

BCS, THE CHARTERED INSTITUTE FOR IT

BCS, The Chartered Institute for IT, is committed to making IT good for society. We use the power of our network to bring about positive, tangible change. We champion the global IT profession and the interests of individuals, engaged in that profession, for the benefit of all.

Exchanging IT expertise and knowledge
The Institute fosters links between experts from industry, academia and business to promote new thinking, education and knowledge sharing.

Supporting practitioners
Through continuing professional development and a series of respected IT qualifications, the Institute seeks to promote professional practice tuned to the demands of business. It provides practical support and information services to its members and volunteer communities around the world.

Setting standards and frameworks
The Institute collaborates with government, industry and relevant bodies to establish good working practices, codes of conduct, skills frameworks and common standards. It also offers a range of consultancy services to employers to help them adopt best practice.

Become a member
Over 70,000 people including students, teachers, professionals and practitioners enjoy the benefits of BCS membership. These include access to an international community, invitations to a roster of local and national events, career development tools and a quarterly thought-leadership magazine. Visit www.bcs.org/membership to find out more.

Further information
BCS, The Chartered Institute for IT,
3 Newbridge Square,
Swindon, SN1 1BY, United Kingdom.
T +44 (0) 1793 417 417
(Monday to Friday, 09:00 to 17:00 UK time)
www.bcs.org/contact
http://shop.bcs.org/

USER EXPERIENCE FOUNDATIONS

Nick de Voil

bcs
The
Chartered
Institute
for IT

Published by BCS Learning and Development Ltd, a wholly owned subsidiary of BCS, The Chartered Institute for IT, 3 Newbridge Square, Swindon, SN1 1BY, UK.
www.bcs.org

Paperback ISBN: 978-1-78017-3498
PDF ISBN: 978-1-78017-3504
ePUB ISBN: 978-1-78017-3511
Kindle ISBN: 978-1-78017-3528

Ebook available

British Cataloguing in Publication Data.
A CIP catalogue record for this book is available at the British Library.

Publisher's acknowledgements
Reviewers: David Travis, Peter Morgan, Leo Poll
Publisher: Ian Borthwick
Commissioning editor: Rebecca Youé
Production manager: Florence Leroy
Project manager: Sunrise Setting Ltd
Copy-editor: Gillian Bourn
Proofreader: Barbara Eastman
Indexer: Matthew Gale
Cover design: Alex Wright
Cover image: Thinkstock © Digital Vision
Typeset by Lapiz Digital Services, Chennai, India

CONTENTS

LIST OF FIGURES AND TABLES

AUTHOR

Nick de Voil is an information systems consultant specialising in helping organisations to design and implement people-oriented processes and systems. His three decades of experience have been gained largely with international capital markets participants, UK public sector bodies and internet startups. A strong believer in breaking down barriers between professional disciplines, Nick has close links with several different communities of practice. At the time of writing he is president of the UK chapter of the International Institute for Business Analysis, a Certified Management Consultant, a Chartered Member of the Institute for Securities and Investment, and a member of BCS, The Chartered Institute for IT, the User Experience Professionals Association, the Business Architecture Guild, the Data Management Association and the Institute of Consulting. Nick is a popular public speaker and has trained hundreds of professionals in user experience, business analysis, project management and requirements engineering.

Nick has an MSc in Human-Computer Interaction with Ergonomics from UCLIC, the University College London Interaction Centre.

FOREWORD

There are few roles in digital design as misunderstood as the discipline of user experience. To some, it means designing user interfaces so that they are pleasant to use. To others, it means providing signposts so that a digital product is simple to navigate. Still others view user experience as the process of understanding user needs.

The discipline of user experience is about all of these, and more. But without a syllabus and a professional qualification to define the scope of the field, it risks being misunderstood and misinterpreted.

Until now.

The book you are now holding is the first of its kind. It describes the content in the BCS Foundation Certificate in User Experience. With a syllabus based on the international standard, ISO 9241-210 'Human-Centred Design for Interactive Systems', BCS defined the professional scope of user experience. By attaining the BCS Foundation Certificate in User Experience, you will be able to:

- Ensure systems have an early and continual focus on users and their tasks.
- Plan and carry out empirical measurements of user behaviour.
- Practise validated learning through prototyping and iterative design.

To attain these goals, you will need to prove you understand both user experience research and user experience design. This means knowing how to carry out contextual user research and how to run usability testing. It also means understanding information architecture, interaction design and visual design. This makes the syllabus of the BCS Foundation Certificate in User Experience both broad and challenging.

There are several books that cover the research component of user experience. And there are many others that describe the design component of the field. But few books successfully integrate these components in a single volume. Nick de Voil has done exactly that with the book you hold in your hands.

I have used the comprehensive syllabus that Nick outlines in this book to train thousands of user researchers and designers in the field of user experience. Many of my students have gone on to have successful careers in user experience and you can do it too. I wish you the best of luck.

Dr David Travis
Director
Userfocus

ACKNOWLEDGEMENTS

I would like to thank everyone who has been involved with the development of the BCS Foundation Certificate in User Experience. In particular I am grateful to Dr David Travis for his significant assistance and guidance with this book. I also want to acknowledge the kind advice on international standards given to me by the late Nigel Bevan.

Becky Youe and Ian Borthwick at BCS have been models of forbearance and encouragement throughout the book's long gestation. Thank you, Becky and Ian! In addition, I am indebted to BCS for allowing the use of the sample exam material.

Thanks to all those who have encouraged me by word and example to set out on this journey and persevere with it, in particular Drs Penny Pullan and Mike Goodland and Adrian Reed. Heartfelt thanks also to the lecturers at UCLIC who taught me so much about human–computer interaction and ergonomics, and to my colleagues and students, too numerous to name individually, who have taught me even more.

Above all, thank you to my wife Nina for her patience and support.

Nick de Voil

ABBREVIATIONS

AEIOU	activities, environments, interactions, objects, users
CX	customer experience
DSDM	Dynamic Systems Development Method
EA	enterprise architecture
GUI	graphical user interface
HCD	human-centred design
HCI	human–computer interaction
HTML	Hypertext Markup Language
HTML5	HTML version 5
IA	information architecture
IEC	International Electrotechnical Commission
IEEE	Institute of Electrical and Electronics Engineers
ISO	International Organization for Standardization
IxD	interaction design
LATCH	location, alphabet, time, category, hierarchy
MECE	mutually exclusive, collectively exhaustive
PACT	people, activities, contexts, technologies
PARC	proximity, alignment, repetition, contrast
SFIA	Skills Framework for the Information Age
SUS	System Usability Scale
UCD	user-centred design
UI	user interface
UML	Unified Modeling Language
UX	user experience
W3C	World Wide Web Consortium
WAI	Web Accessibility Initiative
WCAG	Web Content Accessibility Guidelines

GLOSSARY

A/B testing: A technique used to compare two alternative designs of a live **interactive system** with a large number of **users**.

Accessibility: The **usability** of a product, service, environment or facility by people with the widest range of capabilities (ISO 9241-171).

Accuracy: The extent to which an actual outcome matches an intended outcome (ISO 9241-11).

Affinity diagram: A method used by design teams to organise large amounts of **qualitative research** data and information into groups so that the data can be analysed.

Affordance: The properties of an object that suggest to people how the object can be interacted with; the kind of interaction that is so suggested. Compare **signifier**.

Alignment: The placing of graphical **user interface** elements so that they share horizontal or vertical coordinates.

Assumption persona: A **persona** developed without user research.

Boomerang technique: Answering a question with another question.

Card sort: A research method where participants organise features, functions or pages of a **user interface** into groups that make sense to the participants.

Closed card sort: A **card sort** where the categories into which information can be sorted have been predefined.

Closed question: A question where the participant must choose an answer from among a proposed list of responses. No answer other than the ones proposed is allowed.

Completeness: The extent to which **users** are able to achieve all intended outcomes (ISO 9241-11).

Conceptual model: A model representing the system structure and logical architecture envisaged by the designer of an **interactive system**.

Context of use: The **users**, goals and tasks, resources, and the technical, physical, social, cultural and organisational environments in which a product is used.

Contextual inquiry: A research method where a researcher carries out a site visit to observe **users** carrying out their normal activities in their natural environment.

Contrast: A visual design technique where the object of attention is made very different from the other elements that surround it.

Design pattern: A re-usable solution to a commonly occurring design problem.

Diary study: A **longitudinal research** method where users keep track of the activities in which they engage.

Discount usability: An approach to **usability** that seeks to optimise usability methods for cost-effectiveness.

Effectiveness: The **accuracy** and **completeness** with which **users** achieve specified **goals**. Compare **efficiency** (ISO 9241-11).

Efficiency: The resources used in relation to the results achieved (ISO 9241-11).

Empathy map: A visual summary of what the user hears, sees, thinks and feels within the **context of use**.

Ethnography: The scientific description of people and cultures with their customs, habits and mutual differences.

Eye tracking: A technique used to measure either the point of gaze (where the user is looking) or the motion of the **user's** eye relative to the head.

Fidelity: When used to refer to a **prototype**, this refers to the degree of exactness with which the prototype reproduces the final design. Note that a prototype can have high visual fidelity but low interactive fidelity (for example, static screens created in a graphics program), and low visual fidelity but high interactive fidelity (for example, a paper prototype).

Fitts' law: The time taken to move to a target is a function of the target size and the distance to the target.

Fixation: The pause of an eye movement on a specific area of the visual field.

Formative usability test: A type of iterative **usability** testing that aims to find problems with a system so they can be fixed.

Functional properties: Inherent properties of a software product that determine what the software is able to do: generally concerned with transformation of input data to output data (ISO/IEC 25010).

Functional requirement: A **requirement** specifying **functional properties** of a system.

Gaze plot: A moment-by-moment representation of a **user's** eye movement across the screen.

Goal: An intended outcome (ISO 9241-11).

Heat map: A representation of the different areas of the screen where the **user** has spent the most time looking.

Heuristic: A guideline for evaluating the **usability** of a **user interface**.

Hick's law: The time taken to make a decision increases as the number of choices is expanded.

High-fidelity prototype: A **prototype** that appears very similar to the final system.

Implementation model: The view of the system from the developers' point of view, often with system models and so on.

Indirect user: A person who receives output from a **system**, but does not interact with the system (ISO/IEC 25010).

Information architecture: The discipline that ensures **users** can find the functions, features or content they need to achieve their **tasks**.

Interaction design: The practice of identifying design solutions and creating **prototype user interfaces**.

Interactive system: A combination of hardware and/or software and/or services and/or people that **users** interact with in order to achieve specific **goals** (ISO 9241-11).

Interface control: An element of interaction in a graphical **user interface**, such as a button or scroll bar.

Interface pattern: See **design pattern**.

Iterative design: A design method based on a cyclical process of **prototyping**, testing, analysing and refining a **system**. Based on the results of testing the most recent iteration of a design, changes and refinements are made.

Leading question: An interview question phrased in such a way that it tends to suggest the desired answer.

Longitudinal research: Research that collects data from the same individual(s) over an extended period of time.

Low-fidelity prototype: A **prototype** that has some characteristics of the target system but is otherwise simple, usually in order to produce the prototype and test broad concepts quickly.

Mental model: The internal, mental representation that a user has about how an **interactive system** works.

Microcopy: Text labels that appear on buttons, dialog names, form fields and tooltips.

Moderated usability test: A usability test where a test administrator is with a test participant in real time (whether physically present or not), for example, to remind the participant to think aloud.

Moderator: The person who runs a usability test. The moderator is responsible for ensuring the smooth running of the session and for ensuring that the test objectives are addressed.

Monothetic agglomerative cluster analysis: A statistical method of analysing results of a card sorting session.

Multivariate testing: Generalised version of **A/B testing**, where there are more than two alternatives.

Negative persona: A **persona** representing **users** whom the service is specifically not designed to serve.

Non-functional requirement: A **requirement** specifying properties of a system that are not **functional properties**.

Observation: In the context of a **usability** test, this is something the participant says or does (as distinguished from an 'interpretation', which is the observer's belief about the cause).

Open card sort: A **card sort** where users can create their own grouping scheme.

Open question: A question that cannot be answered 'Yes' or 'No' but requires the participant to answer with a sentence or two.

Paper prototype: A **prototyping** technique that involves creating drawings (often roughly drawn) of a **user interface** that can be used to test out design ideas with end users. There is often the ability to 'interact' with the prototype.

Persona: A fictitious person created to model and describe the **goals**, needs and characteristics of a specific type or group of users.

Primary persona: The main target for the design of the service.

Primary user: A person who interacts with the product (ISO 25010).

Progressive disclosure: An interaction design technique that helps to maintain the focus of a **user's** attention by reducing clutter, confusion and cognitive workload. This improves usability by presenting only the minimum information required for the **task** at hand.

Prototype: Representation of all or part of an **interactive system** that, although limited in some way, can be used for analysis, design and evaluation (ISO 9241-210); to create and use such representations.

Proximity: A visual design technique used to organise and group the various parts of a **user interface**.

Qualitative research: Analysis of motivations, patterns of thought, opinion, attitude, assessment or behaviour (ISO 20252).

Quantitative research: The numerical representation of observations for the purpose of describing and explaining phenomena that those observations reflect (ISO 20252).

Recall question: A question that requires the participant to remember an event that has happened in the past.

Repetition: A visual design technique used to create consistency and to add visual interest.

Requirement: (1) A condition or capability needed by a user to solve a problem or achieve an objective. (2) A condition or capability that must be met or possessed by a system or system component to satisfy a contract, standard, specification or other formally imposed documents. (3) A documented representation of a condition or capability as in (1) or (2) (IEEE 610.12-1990).

Saccade: The movement of the eye from one part of the visual field to another.

Sample size: The number of participants interviewed or observed and so on in a given research study.

Satisfaction: The extent to which the user's physical, cognitive and emotional responses that result from the use of a system, product or service meet the user's needs and expectations (ISO 9241-11).

Scrum: A product development framework, falling within the 'Agile' set of methods. Attributed to Ken Schwaber.

Signifier: An indicator of how something is designed to be interacted with to get an intended result. Compare **affordance**.

Sketch: A design concept or solution not intended for testing with **users**.

Stakeholder: An individual or organisation having a right, share, claim or interest in a system or in its possession of characteristics that meet their needs and expectations (ISO 15288).

Summative usability test: A type of **usability** testing that aims to measure usability metrics, such as **effectiveness**, **efficiency** and **satisfaction**.

System: A combination of interacting elements organised to achieve one or more stated purposes (ISO 25010).

Task: Physical or cognitive activities required to achieve a **goal** (ISO 9241-11).

Thinking aloud: A technique from cognitive interviewing where a participant describes his or her thought processes when engaged in an activity.

Unmoderated usability test: A usability test where the test participant works alone on the test tasks, for example, from their home computer.

Usability: The extent to which a system, product or service can be used by specified **users** to achieve specified **goals** with **effectiveness**, **efficiency** and **satisfaction** in a specified **context of use** (ISO 9241-11).

Usability inspection: A **usability** evaluation process where an expert evaluates a design against a set of usability principles or standards.

User: Person who interacts with a product (or system or service) (ISO 9241-11); individual or group that interacts with a system or benefits from a system during its utilisation (ISO 25010).

User acceptance test: A test conducted to determine if the functional requirements of a specification have been met.

User-centred design: A design process in which the needs, wants and limitations of the end users of a product, service or process are considered at each stage of design.

User experience: A person's perceptions and responses resulting from the use or anticipated use of a product, system or service (ISO 9241-210).

User group: A subset of intended **users** who are differentiated from other intended users by characteristics of the users, **tasks** or environments that could influence **usability** (ISO 9241-11).

User interface: All components of an **interactive system** that provide information and controls for the **user** to accomplish specific **tasks** with the interactive system (ISO 9241-110).

User journey map: A diagram showing the steps in a scenario in which a user interacts with a **system** or service.

User need: In UK government terminology, a user objective expressed in **user story** format.

User research: The process of uncovering **user** needs, **goals** and motivations.

User story: User stories are part of an agile approach that helps to shift the focus from writing about requirements to talking about them. All Agile user stories include a written sentence or two and, more importantly, a series of conversations about desired functionality. The most common general format is 'As a [user role] I need/want to [do this task] so that [I can achieve this goal].'

Validated learning: A form of iterative design where the design team test design hypotheses with **users**.

Visual design: The practice of devising grids, laying out pages, choosing colour palettes and developing icons.

Wireframe: An image, or set of images, which displays the functional elements of a website or page, typically used for planning a site's structure and functionality.

1 INTRODUCTION

This book introduces the professional discipline of user experience (UX) at a foundational level. It describes what UX professionals do, why they do it and why it works. The book is designed as a companion guide to the BCS Foundation Certificate in User Experience, and its structure is closely modelled on the certificate's syllabus, available at: bcs.org/ux

As well as explaining the most important techniques and practices of UX, I discuss the field's underlying principles, and we look at the ways in which UX fits in with other disciplines and project approaches.

This book is for anyone who wants to develop their understanding of user experience. People who will find this book useful might include:

- Experienced UX professionals who want to acquire the BCS Foundation Certificate in User Experience, and need a quick guide to its scope and philosophy.

- UX professionals at an early stage of their career who would value a clear and simple overview of the field.

- People at the beginning of their career who are considering UX as a career option.

- IT professionals who are currently working within a non-UX field of specialisation, such as software development, testing, business analysis or project management, and who are considering a move into UX.

- Non-IT professionals who are considering a move into UX.

- Non-UX IT professionals who are not considering a career move, but who would like to understand the field better so that they can work more effectively with UX specialists.

- Non-UX IT professionals who are not considering a career move, but who would like to extend and enrich their practice by learning about UX.

UX is a comparatively young discipline. Like other young disciplines, it is characterised by a lack of uniformity in principles, terminology and methods. To some extent this is a positive sign of a lively and diverse professional community that is constantly developing and reflecting on its practice. Sometimes, however, there is a risk that inexperienced readers will find themselves misled or confused by material on the web or elsewhere that repeats misconceptions and fallacies about UX, or which overstates partisan positions on certain issues. This book aims to provide readers with a solid base for the development of their knowledge about the field. In cases where there is doubt or disagreement, the book relies on the following sources, in order of decreasing importance:

1. The definitions, principles and processes defined in international standards, especially ISO 9241-210 (2019) and ISO 9241-11 (2018).
2. The concepts and terminology incorporated in the syllabus for the BCS Foundation Certificate in User Experience and in its associated exam questions.
3. Generally accepted good practice in the professional UX community.
4. The author's own experience and opinions.

THE BCS FOUNDATION CERTIFICATE IN USER EXPERIENCE

In 2015, BCS, The Chartered Institute for IT, introduced a Foundation Certificate in User Experience.

The syllabus for the exam is available on the BCS website. It is organised into the following sections, with learning objectives for each:

1. Guiding principles
2. User research
3. Illustrating the context of use
4. Measuring usability
5. Information architecture
6. Interaction design
7. Visual design
8. User interface prototyping
9. Usability evaluation

The organisation of this book from Chapters 3 to 11 follows this structure exactly. Additionally, supplementary chapters (1, 2 and 12) have been included at the beginning and end to provide some orientation and further useful information, particularly with a view to the needs of the groups of prospective readers mentioned above. For readers who are thinking of taking the Foundation Certificate exam, it is important to realise that the supplementary chapters do not form part of the syllabus and are not 'examinable'. There are also some sections in Chapters 3 to 11 containing non-examinable material. These are clearly marked (see the 'Visual cues in this book' section, below).

The Appendix provides some more information on the Foundation Certificate examination. Appendix A1 describes the *K level* scheme, which governs the allocation of a specified level to each learning objective.

Each chapter starts with an introductory section indicating the topics covered, followed by a table that lists the learning objectives for the chapter as defined by the syllabus.

Each learning objective is at one of three levels: Remember (the most basic), Understand or Apply (the most advanced). At the end of each examinable chapter are some sample questions, with answers and explanations.

There's more to UX than what's in this book!

Each section of the syllabus for the BCS Foundation Certificate in User Experience defines several learning objectives relating to the area in question. To maintain its focus, this book restricts itself to covering the subject matter of the given learning objectives for each area, and providing contextual information around them. In practice, the scope of each area is wider than is suggested by the learning objectives; the book therefore omits a great deal of information.

For example, the chapter on information architecture does not discuss search strategy in detail; the chapter on interaction design does not explore the range of input and output methods and devices that are currently available; and the chapter on visual design barely scratches the surface of practical graphic design. Arguably, there are some entire top-level areas that could have been added, on content design, for example.

The further reading section at the end of each chapter provides signposts to additional useful information.

INTERNATIONAL STANDARDS

As well as giving guidance on methods, international standards provide commonly agreed definitions of basic terms and concepts. We will use them as a reference point in this book to help us find our way through the sometimes conflicting or unclear terminology used by different practitioners.

ISO 9241

The most important standard in the field of user experience is ISO 9241, whose overall title is, at the time of writing, 'Ergonomics of human-system interaction'. This is in fact a family of interrelated documents, each of which evolves over time. Many of them have been given new numbers in recent years, or will soon be given new numbers.

The two parts of ISO 9241 most relevant to this book are ISO 9241-210 (2019), 'Human-Centred Design for Interactive Systems', which sets out the principles and process described in Chapter 3, and ISO 9241-11 (2018), 'Usability: definitions and concepts', which contains operational definitions of usability and its components. We will also refer to several other standards from the International Organization for Standardization (ISO) and other bodies in passing.

VISUAL CUES IN THIS BOOK

Terms defined in the Glossary

Where a word other than a heading or subheading is printed as **bold text** in this book, this means that the term is defined in the Glossary.

Boxes

On many pages you will see 'box-outs', shaded areas with an icon in the margin. The intention of the box-outs is to draw your attention to particularly important points. The icons are used as follows:

Golden Rule
An important UX rule or principle that you need to know in order to achieve the BCS Foundation Certificate in UX.

Definition
A definition that you need to know in order to achieve the BCS Foundation Certificate in UX. The definitions are all contained in the Glossary, but some of the most important are repeated in the main body of the book.

Bright Idea
A particularly noteworthy practical tip.

Danger
This alerts you to a possible misconception that could cause confusion. These are often to do with potentially misleading use of terminology. Special attention is paid to 'false friends' – terms that may be familiar to readers from other contexts, but which are used in a different sense in UX.

Remember
Something you need to pay attention to in order to get the best out of the book.

Extra information
Information that you do *not* need to know in order to achieve the BCS Foundation Certificate in UX. This material supplements the syllabus but does not form part of it.

REFERENCES

ISO 9241-11:2018 (2018) *Ergonomics of Human-System Interaction – Part 11: Usability: Definitions and Concepts.* International Organization for Standardization (ISO), Geneva.

ISO 9241-210:2019 (2019) *Ergonomics of Human-System Interaction – Part 210: Human-Centred Design for Interactive Systems.* International Organization for Standardization (ISO), Geneva.

FURTHER READING

Halvorson, K. and Rach, M. (2012) *Content Strategy for the Web*, 2nd edn. New Riders, Berkeley, CA.

Kortum, P. (2008) *HCI beyond the GUI: Design for Haptic, Speech, Olfactory, and Other Nontraditional Interfaces*. Elsevier, Burlington, MA.

Redish, J.G. (2012) *Letting Go of the Words: Writing Web Content that Works*. Morgan Kaufmann, San Francisco, CA.

2 THE CONTEXT FOR UX (1)
Rationale and Concepts

What sort of thing is happening here?

Cutting Edge, Graham Taylor (1994)

INTRODUCTION

This chapter discusses:

- What sort of thing is user experience?
- How does UX relate to customer experience, usability, accessibility, user-centred design, human-centred design and service design?
- What is the business case for UX?
- Why is UX important?
- Why is UX different?

WHAT SORT OF THING IS UX?

At the most fundamental level, the term 'user experience' means exactly what it says. That is, as ISO 9241-210 (2019) puts it:

[A person's] perceptions and responses that result from the use and/or anticipated use of a system, product or service.

As this suggests, user experience at the most basic level is a set of subjective *psychological events and states* (perceptions) experienced by an individual and immediately accessible only to the person in question. We may gain an insight into those events and states by seeing how the individual *speaks and (re)acts* (their responses).

Another definition, by the Nielsen Norman Group (n.d.), takes a more objective and impersonal perspective: 'All aspects of the end-user's interaction with the company, its services, and its products'.

Although this formulation has not moved far from the first one, the focus has moved away from the individual's inner world, towards an observable set of interactions. The user's own subjective point of view is just one part of an overall reality, all of which is amenable to objective analysis. This small shift in perspective has significant implications. If we can describe and analyse elements of the user's experience objectively, we may also be able to influence that experience in a controlled way. However, it would be going too far to suggest that we can 'design' a person's experience. The most we can hope for is to design parts of the context within which that experience takes place.

Key elements of UX

We can see five key elements in the definitions above:

- A *person* – that is, the user.
- A *system*, whether viewed comparatively narrowly as a product or software application, or more broadly as a service, organisation or brand.
- *Use* of, or *interaction* with, the system by the person.
- The *perceptions* of the person resulting from their use of the system. These are mainly psychological phenomena, potentially of some complexity, but might also stem from physiological factors. For example, they might include some kind of physical discomfort resulting from use of the system, or a feeling of frustration induced by the physical difficulty of operating the system's interface.
- The person's responses resulting from their use of the system. While internal emotional responses are relatively hard for an observer to detect and analyse, many responses are behavioural and can be clearly seen in the person's *actions*.

These elements can be seen graphically in Figure 2.1. Note that the 'system', even if it exists most obviously as a technical artefact, such as a piece of hardware or software, always contains other elements such as people, services, rules, procedures, cultural assumptions and so on. These elements are sometimes overlooked but often play a decisive part in the nature and quality of the user's experience.

Figure 2.1 Basic model of UX

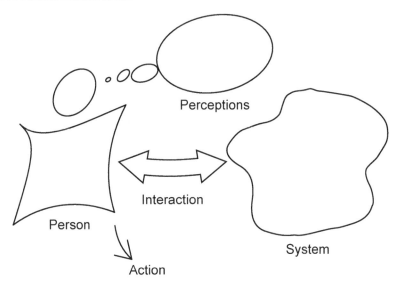

Products, services and systems

In this book, we will sometimes refer to 'products', 'services' or 'systems'. Wherever one of those terms in used, the discussion is equally relevant to products, services or socio-technical systems in the broadest sense. The applicability of the principles described is much wider than a single product. A mobile app, an enterprise IT system or a call centre-based support service would all be examples; equally, an entire organisation, or a service provided by one or more organisations, can and should be considered a system from the perspective of the customers' experience. Although human-centred design originated as a way of designing individual artefacts, it is equally powerful when applied to systems on a larger scale.

Similarly, when we refer to the **user interface**, we are not just talking about a software system's input and output of data via a screen, speakers or microphones. It can include conversations with people, information that is displayed on posters or disseminated through advertisements, the physical delivery of goods and so on.

All these types of products and services can be thought of as examples of what ISO 9241-11 (2018) calls an **interactive system**, defined as 'a combination of hardware and/or software and/or services and/or people that **users** interact with in order to achieve specific **goals**'.

The key elements of UX in more detail

Why are we interested in the nature of someone's experience of a product? The answer, of course, is that we want to make it better in some way – or, if the product does not yet exist, to design the product so that the experience will be a good one. To support that aim, we first need to expand our basic model of UX to include some more elements.

Intentions: goals and tasks

First, the person's use of the system does not happen by chance. There is a reason for it. People are purposeful creatures. They interact with software systems or companies because they want something; the interaction is a means to an end. The system's usability and the quality of the user's experience cannot be evaluated without taking the user's purposes or intentions into account.

It is helpful to distinguish between two kinds of intention, most commonly referred to as **goals** and **tasks**. The user's goals are the outcomes that they want to achieve, and they believe engaging with the system may help them to attain those goals. Tasks are the things that the user needs to do in order to achieve their goal. If we are creating a new technical solution to help people achieve a particular goal, we will first study and understand the tasks that they must currently carry out to that end, and later we will design new tasks that will result in the goal being reached in a different but better way. At a lower level of detail, we can identify individual cognitive or motor *operations* making up the task that must be carried out using the interface that we are creating. Donald A. Norman (2005) suggests a four-level task hierarchy composed of activities, tasks, actions and operations. As Alan Cooper et al. (2014) point out, these are all subordinate to goals.

Goals and tasks are common-sense ideas that map easily onto the concepts of the same name in requirements engineering, business analysis and systems analysis. Other words that are sometimes used for goals are *aims*, *objectives* or *needs*. A more troublesome near-synonym is *requirement*, which we will discuss later in this chapter and in Chapters 3 and 5. A near-synonym for tasks is *activities*.

Goals are discussed further in Chapters 4 and 5, where we consider different ways of classifying and documenting them.

Predispositions

Second, we must acknowledge that we can only hope to gain a good understanding of the user's perceptions and responses if we are prepared to investigate and model their subjective world in some way. People vary, and we need to think carefully about the ways in which they vary in order to identify groups whose needs we will try to meet, and groups whose needs we will not try to meet. Interaction with a system is reflexive: in other words, not only is each user predisposed to perceive their interaction with the system in a particular way, but also the experience of the interaction will modify those predispositions and influence their future perceptions (see Figure 2.2).

Figure 2.2 Extended model of UX

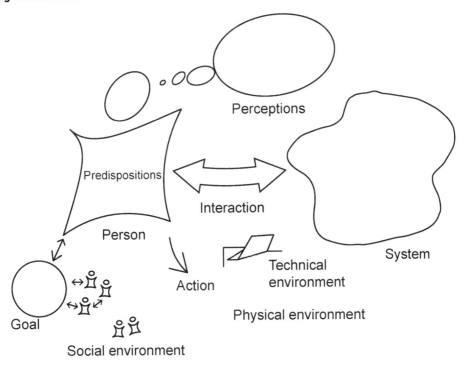

Attributes of people that we may need to model include (but are not limited to) experience, knowledge, skills, attitudes, motivations, values, expectations and dispositions, as well as their physical abilities. In Chapters 4 and 5 we discuss how to do this.

Environment
Third, use of a system does not happen in a vacuum. The physical environment in which the interaction takes place will impose constraints on the design. Systems are often created on the basis of assumptions about the environment or a relationship to it. These assumptions may not be well-founded. For example, a designer working in a comfortable studio may forget that the user could be in an environment with noteworthy levels of temperature, light, humidity, space, movement, noise or stress. The user may be unable to speak the local language, or to speak at all. The user may be unable to perform the motor or cognitive operations required by the design.

One aspect of the environment that is often particularly important to designers is the *technical* environment – the set of tools with which the user engages, or which constrain and influence their behaviour.

Social setting and structure
Fourth, although the classical model in human–computer interaction is of one person interacting with one computer, this does not capture the complexity of the real world. In particular, we often need to pay attention to the fact that the user is working as part of a *social group* of some sort. Very often there will be structure associated with the group, as in the case of a department within an organisation.

The concept of goals is useful in thinking about this situation. To the extent that they can be agreed on, whether explicitly or implicitly, some goals are shared by multiple individuals within an organisation. While tasks are best thought of as something relating to one individual at any given time, shared goals are part of people's shared reality and can help us to design for successful user experience in an organisational setting.

The social setting may also include other people who do not share the user's goals. Indeed, they may have other goals that are in conflict with the user's goals.

These further elements of UX are reflected in Figure 2.2.

WHO IS THE 'USER'?

As we have seen, we generally refer to the people whose needs we are concerned with meeting as **users**. Accordingly, ISO 25010 (2011) defines a user as any 'individual or group that interacts with a system or benefits from a system during its utilisation'. This definition covers a wide spectrum of ways in which people can relate to a system. ISO 9241-210 (2019) uses the term 'human-centred' rather than 'user-centred', emphasising that it is not just direct users of the system whose perspective must be taken into account.

ISO 25010 (2011) makes a distinction between *direct* and *indirect* users. Direct users are people who interact with the system. Indirect users do not interact with the system, but receive output from it.

Direct users can be divided into *primary* and *secondary* users. The primary users of the system are the people who use it to support their achievement of primary goals, whereas secondary users only interact with the system in the course of providing some kind of support function.

It is worth noting that there are also often people who benefit from a system during its utilisation who neither interact with it nor receive output from it – for example, shareholders in a software company.

Stakeholders

Equally, there are people whose perspective needs to be taken into account in designing a system besides those who benefit from it during its utilisation. The concept of **stakeholders** is useful here. ISO 15288 (ISO/IEC/IEEE 15288, 2015) defines a stakeholder as 'an individual or organisation having a right, share, claim or interest in a system or in its possession of characteristics that meet their needs and expectations'. This includes anyone to whom the system represents an opportunity or a threat – for example, competitors.

Two meanings of 'stakeholder'

A **stakeholder** is any individual or organisation having an interest in a system or its characteristics (ISO/IEC/IEEE 15288, 2015).

A **user**, in the narrowest definition, is a person who interacts with the system (ISO 9241-210, 2019).

To be strictly accurate, then, users are a subset of stakeholders. All users are stakeholders, but not all stakeholders are users.

In a UX context, 'stakeholders' is often used (for example, by Garrett, 2010 and Goodwin, 2011) to mean exclusively 'business stakeholders', as distinct from users, that is, people who have a business interest in the system but who are specifically *not* its users.

Figure 2.3 shows how the different categories of users and stakeholders relate to each other. There are two important points to be made regarding this hierarchy.

From a project management and marketing point of view, the chances of project success will be improved if the perspectives of all the stakeholder groups are considered.

However, to create a good product, it is absolutely essential that the design should be guided by the needs of the primary users, without it being compromised by the preferences, opinions or prejudices of other stakeholder groups.

Figure 2.3 Users and stakeholders

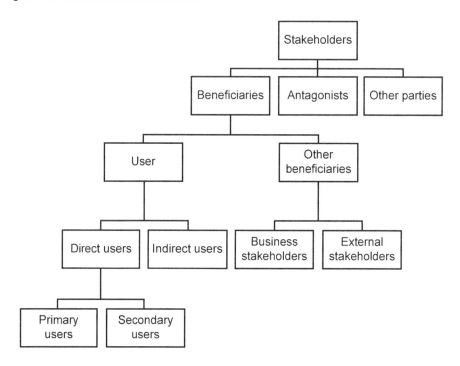

If truth be told, the terms 'user-centred' and 'human-centred' sometimes describe an aspiration rather than reality. A project is only truly human-centred when it is focused on meeting the users' needs without regard to the type of solution. In practice, when design teams are working on a product, the thing that is often really at the centre of the stage – even when it does not yet exist – is the product itself. A more accurate term in these cases might be 'people-oriented design' (de Voil, 2013). In any human-centred design process, the users and other stakeholders are decisively important, and the whole process is oriented towards them.

UX AND USABILITY

The ISO standards have tried to keep the concepts of UX and usability distinct from each other, by stressing objectively measurable factors in the definition of usability while emphasising the subjective nature of experience in the definition of UX. However, most practitioners would agree that UX is the broader concept and that usability is a part of the overall user experience. Usability is discussed in detail in Chapter 6.

UX AND ACCESSIBILITY

As mentioned earlier, people vary. We need to avoid accidentally or deliberately designing systems that are difficult or impossible for some people to use because of assumptions that are built into them about users' physiological or cognitive attributes. This is harder than it sounds, because making assumptions about other people is a fundamental and normal thing for human beings to do. **Accessibility**, discussed further in Chapter 11, is the property of a product or system that refers to this. The key to creating accessible systems is *inclusive design*, discussed further in Chapter 3.

Often there is a need to design a digital service, that is, a service that is accessed over the internet. To most users, digital services offer compelling advantages, such as convenience, speed, choice and low cost. However, there may be some users of the service who are unable to access it unaided, if at all. This may be because of physical or cognitive disabilities, learning difficulties, language skills or simply lack of access to technology or the ability to use it. To ensure that these users are not excluded from using the service, it needs to include appropriate *assisted digital support*. This means helping people to use the digital service by providing support, for example in person, on the telephone or via web chat. It is an alternative to designing separate versions of the service, delivered over different channels, for different classes of user.

EXTENDED MEANINGS OF 'USER EXPERIENCE'

The term 'user experience' suffers from a bad case of *metonymy*, the practice whereby people use a word to refer by extension to something different but related. This is one of the reasons why discussions about UX often seem to go around in circles with no evident progress towards mutual understanding. As summarised in Figure 2.4, 'UX' is used to refer to all of the following:

- A set of *professional practices*. We might say that someone is 'doing UX'.
- A professional *community* including people who are employed in a more or less well-understood set of roles, such as user researcher, information architect or interaction designer.
- A set of specific *techniques* that are used, such as contextual observation or usability testing.
- The set of *competencies* that someone using those techniques or employed in one of those roles needs, for example, usability test moderation or interaction design.
- A set of *work products* that are typically produced by people engaged in user experience design, such as persona descriptions or wireframes.
- A *mindset*. A colleague might say that someone is 'not really doing UX' because she believes they are paying lip-service to UX practices without wholeheartedly subscribing to our view of the authentic UX philosophy.
- An *organisational unit*, whether in the general sense of a function that is to be found in many organisations, or in the particular sense of the specific individuals employed by that function in one organisation.
- An *academic discipline*. The academic discipline relating to UX is more often referred to as human–computer interaction (HCI).

Figure 2.4 Possible meanings of 'user experience'

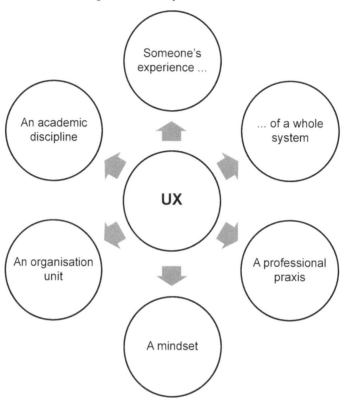

MISLEADING USES OF 'USER EXPERIENCE'

'UX' is also sometimes used with the intention of denoting an intrinsic attribute of a product or system, as in: 'This app has a poor user experience.' Strictly speaking, this is an inappropriate use of the term. As we have seen already, the user's experience is a phenomenon that emerges from the interaction between the user and the product. It is not inherent in the product itself.

Particularly in a recruitment context, the phrase 'UX/UI design' (user experience/user interface) or 'UI/UX design' is often heard. User interface design is actually a sub-discipline of user experience, and so this formulation represents what logicians call a 'category error', which inappropriately seeks to place two concepts on the same level when one is in fact subordinate to the other. It is a particularly pernicious mistake, because its take-up and usage help to perpetuate confusion about the field's basic concepts.

HOW DOES UX RELATE TO OTHER DISCIPLINES?

In this section, we look at the similarities and differences between UX and related disciplines at a high level.

Marketing

For decades, marketing professionals have been attempting to increase sales by understanding customers and their preferences, using tools such as surveys, psychographic profiling, focus groups and Voice of the Customer programmes. Clearly, there is an overlap between the concerns of marketing and UX, and some of the techniques used are superficially very similar. However, the underlying mindset is completely different. The marketing discipline is focused on maximising sales. UX is focused on meeting people's needs. However, UX projects are often sponsored by marketing departments. In these circumstances the UX design team must be prepared to put time and effort into evangelising for the human-centred approach and its associated business benefits.

Customer experience

Customer experience (CX) is a discipline that has developed from marketing. CX professionals analyse and try to optimise the experience of a company's customers over time and with reference to specific touchpoints and channels. Bearing in mind the second definition of UX that we looked at earlier, we can see that CX and UX are similar in their scope and aims. However, the marketing culture and mindset is still evident in CX. To put it simply, marketing is about finding customers for a product, whereas UX is about designing products that will help customers.

As we have seen, there is a wide range of relationships that people may have to a product or service, which come under the general heading of 'user'. A customer relationship is one of these. The customer is the person who makes the purchase decision. By definition, therefore, UX is a broader spectrum than CX because it covers other perspectives besides this.

Business analysis

Business analysts are concerned with finding solutions to business problems. A large part of their work, as well as that of related disciplines such as systems analysis and requirements engineering, is about discovering what users need. The key difference is one of perspective. While business analysts tend to put the needs of the *business stakeholders* first, user experience researchers are primarily focused on the *direct users* and their needs. A distinction is sometimes made between 'business requirements' on the one hand, and 'user needs' on the other. It is fair to say that business analysts are more concerned with the first of these, and user experience researchers with the second. However, the difference can be overstated: business analysts also need to understand user needs, and UX researchers also need to understand business needs.

WHY IS UX IMPORTANT?

If users' experience with a system is bad, then the system is a failure. It may be a technically excellent product from an engineering point of view, but that is of no value if people cannot use it or do not find it an effective way of achieving their goals. User-centred design aims to mitigate this risk.

We also need to consider the bigger picture. As ISO 9241-210 (2019) puts it,

> Products, systems and services should be designed to take account of the people who will use them as well as other stakeholder groups, including those who might be affected (directly or indirectly) by their use ... In modern society, a key issue is to encourage socially responsible designs ... integrating and balancing out the economic, social and environmental considerations.

Technology is woven into the fabric of our lives. Our ways of being, thinking and behaving are framed by socio-technical systems that have come into existence as the cumulative result of a series of small-scale and large-scale decisions made by people working in organisations, often on programmes of work that are conceived as IT projects. In effect, the makers of those decisions are designing the experience of all the individuals affected: not only the individuals who interact directly with the system's technical elements via a user interface (primary users), but the people who are enmeshed in the web of consequences that spreads out, whether by design or not, from the way the system works.

An example of this is provided by companies that offer economic value to users through a business model based on disintermediation via mobile apps. Using an app, you might book holiday accommodation directly with the owner of a property, instead of using the services of existing participants in the holiday accommodation market, such as hotels; or you might book a taxi ride directly with the driver. Is this a simple story of technology meeting an unmet need via the magic of the internet? At first glance, it might look that way, but in fact that is not the case at all. At the core of this situation there is a technical artefact meeting a need, but there are effects that ripple outwards in ever-widening circles, with impacts on the employment market, social and political environment, taxation system and legal system, to name only a few areas.

The business case for UX

The business case for UX can be seen in terms of four levels. These are tactical cost reduction, project risk mitigation, product strategy and dynamic capability management.

At the *cost reduction* level, there are several well-established ways in which UX can reduce costs, for example:

- Saving operational staff costs by enabling staff to carry out tasks more quickly.
- Saving operational staff costs by enabling staff to carry out tasks more accurately, thus saving costs associated with remedying mistakes.
- Saving support staff costs by allowing customers to understand the product or service and use it effectively without help.

- Saving development costs by eliminating the need for custom-built user interfaces to be rebuilt because of usability defects.

At the *risk mitigation* level, UX can contribute by providing a process that greatly increases the probability of a usable and successful product.

UX can play a key role in *product strategy*. Products and services that are usable and genuinely meet people's needs will ultimately – all other things being equal – be more successful in the marketplace and generate more revenue.

At the *capability management* level, UX is about understanding people and developing products and services that people want, through a process that allows the organisation to react to new information on a continual basis.

WHY IS UX DIFFERENT?

A human-centred approach to systems design differs from some more traditional approaches in its structural features – the activities required and the order in which they are performed – which are discussed further in Chapter 3. More importantly, a distinctive mindset is required. Here we pick out some additional underlying themes that go to the heart of why the approach of UX is different.

Relative importance of functionality

In a systems engineering approach to systems design, the most important thing is functionality. 'Non-functional' attributes and constraints such as usability are often considered to be of secondary importance, and consideration of them may be deferred until the scope and features of the system are already defined. Attention may be paid to the system's 'look and feel', but this is overlaid on a design whose structure is driven by features and functionality. Software companies have traditionally competed on functionality; they aim to improve their competitive position by adding features, rather than maintaining their products' level of usability. New features are sometimes chosen for their perceived value as technological innovations, rather than with direct reference to users' needs.

In a human-centred approach, this order of priorities is turned on its head. Usability and usefulness are the most important product attributes, and features are only included if they contribute to those aims.

A concrete way of thinking

In systems analysis, the aim is to identify abstract concepts that can be accurately modelled as data, processes and rules within a computer system. Interaction with stakeholders during a project is implicitly organised to bring about this objective. The specifics of real-life situations are discarded as early as possible in this process. In so far as different individuals can perceive the same situation differently and describe it in differing terms, analysts try to neutralise or overcome that variety of perspectives. Once they have derived a formal model, they can use the tools of logic to develop, implement and test it.

In a human-centred approach, by contrast, we attach great value to the concrete, specific details of the environment that users inhabit and the activities that they carry out. Although we acknowledge that abstraction of concepts and standardisation of vocabulary need to happen eventually, we try to defer that to as late a stage as possible. We actively seek to identify the variety of ways in which different people think about the problem domain, and the range of language that they use to talk about it. A key attribute of many of the techniques described in this book is that they take data derived from multiple viewpoints and go about structuring it in ways that respect the users' authentic ways of thinking, rather than forcing it into a logical form that prematurely takes over the design process.

The time dimension

This abstraction, or removal of context, which is typical of traditional systems analysis, has one particularly noticeable effect: the loss of the time dimension. Processes tend to be seen as islands of logic. The way in which people experience the service over a sustained period of time is often not explicitly modelled; nor is the way that the experience evolves. Too often, the result of this is frustration and inefficiency when the system turns out not to support the sequence of events that unfolds over the course of time.

A user-centred approach puts this right. UX methods use the power of narrative to understand and communicate the way that people really experience things. The time dimension is the final key conceptual element of UX in addition to those shown in Figure 2.2, which shows a snapshot of the situation at one particular moment in time.

Aesthetics and affect

Sometimes people think that UX is about creating attractive visual interfaces. This is basically incorrect. As the rest of this book will make clear, UX is primarily about understanding users and their needs, and designing to make sure that those needs are met.

However, that does not mean aesthetic considerations are insignificant. Arguably, they are important for their own sake; but also there is a considerable body of evidence supporting the view that aesthetically pleasing user interfaces are more usable than others. Self-evidently, a good-looking interface will result in a better user experience. People react more positively to attractive interfaces. This puts them in a frame of mind where they are more prepared to persevere with finding out how to accomplish a task that might not be self-explanatory. Human-centred design takes this into account.

Psychologists distinguish between two different aspects of our interaction with the world: *cognition* and *affect*. Cognition concerns the largely rational process by which we perceive, process and store information. Affect is to do with our emotions and feelings. Conventionally, the design of business systems is largely concerned with supporting cognitive processes in an optimal way. We need to take affect into account as well, most particularly when designing consumer products. This can only be done effectively by including UX design from the start of the process.

SUMMARY

While the principles of user experience are often associated with the design of standalone products such as software apps and websites, they 'scale up' to the design of services and other socio-technical systems.

User experience emerges from the interaction of one or more users with a product or service. It consists of the users' perceptions of, and responses to, the interaction. It both affects and is affected by the users' goals and predispositions. It is strongly influenced by the physical and social environment of the users.

The term 'user experience' is used in a wide variety of ways. The concerns and techniques of the UX discipline are superficially similar to those of marketing and customer experience, but the mindset is very different. The respective primary concerns of UX specialists and business analysts are user needs and business needs, but each must also understand the other perspective.

Human-centred design prioritises usability over features or functionality. Rather than trusting in the expertise of specialists to build abstract models, it is based on understanding and valuing the subjective experience of users. Key aspects of this are user emotional responses and the time dimension.

REFERENCES

Cooper, A., Reimann, R., Cronin, D. and Noessel, C. (2014) *About Face: The Essentials of Interaction Design*. Wiley, Indianapolis, IN.

Cutting Edge, Graham Taylor: The Impossible Job (1994) [TV programme] Channel 4.

de Voil, N. (2013) People-oriented approaches. In Pullan, P. and Archer, J. (eds), *Business Analysis and Leadership: Influencing Change*. Kogan Page, London. Available from: https://www.koganpage.com/download?id=521

Garrett, J.J. (2010) *The Elements of User Experience: User-Centered Design for the Web and Beyond*. Pearson Education, San Francisco, CA.

Goodwin, K. (2011) *Designing for the Digital Age: How to Create Human-Centered Products and Services*. Wiley, Indianapolis, IN.

ISO 9241-11:2018 (2018) *Ergonomics of Human-System Interaction – Part 11: Usability: Definitions and Concepts*. International Organization for Standardization (ISO), Geneva.

ISO 9241-210:2019 (2019) *Ergonomics of Human–System Interaction – Part 210: Human-Centred Design for Interactive Systems*. International Organization for Standardization (ISO), Geneva.

ISO/IEC 25010:2011 (2011) *Systems and Software Engineering – Systems and Software Quality Requirements and Evaluation (SQuaRE) – System and Software Quality Models*. International Organization for Standardization (ISO), Geneva.

ISO/IEC/IEEE 15288:2015 (2015) *Systems and Software Engineering – System Life Cycle Processes*. International Organization for Standardization (ISO), Geneva.

Nielsen Norman Group (no date) *The Definition of User Experience.* Available from: https://www.nngroup.com/articles/definition-user-experience/

Norman, D.A. (2005) Human-centered design considered harmful. *interactions*, 12(4), 14–19.

FURTHER READING

Downe, L. (2019) *Good Services: How to Design Services that Work.* BIS Publishers, Amsterdam.

Norman, D.A. (2004) *Emotional Design: Why We Love (or Hate) Everyday Things.* Basic Civitas Books, New York.

Travis, D. (2007) *A Business Case for Usability.* Available from: https://www.userfocus. co.uk/articles/usabilitybenefits.html

3 GUIDING PRINCIPLES

Do not do unto others as you would that they should do unto you. Their tastes may not be the same.

George Bernard Shaw (1903)

INTRODUCTION

This chapter explains what user-centred design is. We start by considering design itself, and looking at some of the ways in which design is commonly neglected or marginalised. We then move on to look at the principles and processes of the human-centred design cycle as defined in ISO 9241-210 (2019). We identify what is special about user-centred design, and review the concepts of inclusive design, user experience, usability and user acceptance testing.

LEARNING OBJECTIVES

After reading this chapter you will be able to:

Remember	• Recall ISO 9241 as an important standard in the field of usability
	• Recall the difference between usability and user experience
	• Recall the difference between usability and user acceptance testing
Understand	• Articulate the importance of taking the user's perspective
	• Paraphrase the key principles of user-centred design
	• Have an understanding of different user perspectives and goals for using a system
	• Summarise the benefits of inclusive design

THE PLACE OF DESIGN IN THE PROJECT PROCESS

Many products and systems are hard to use, or are not found to be useful. Consequently they cause their users frustration or worse, and in a business context, they waste money. How can we design systems that are usable and useful? This book is about a particular approach to designing products, systems and services which aims to achieve just that. As a first step, we need to be clear what 'design' means. There are two specific traps to avoid here.

First, anyone who is familiar with the 'system development life cycle' concept – see, for example, Cadle (2014) – will be familiar with the notion of design as one stage or component in the overall project process, whose exact nature depends on the type of life cycle being used, but which generally is logically or chronologically consequent upon requirements analysis. In this book, we use 'design' in a different sense: to refer to the entire project process (as in, for example, Beyer and Holtzblatt, 1997; Newman and Lamming, 1995).

Second, in colloquial speech we often talk about 'design' when referring to the cosmetic aspects of a product. The scope of user-centred design is, however, certainly not restricted to cosmetic elements. Design is the whole project.

'Design' is the whole project

We use the word 'design' to refer to the entire process of understanding users' needs, conceiving a response to them and specifying all aspects of the solution's function and form. Design is not restricted to one part of the life cycle or one section of the team.

Inescapably, all products and systems are designed. Design is nothing more or less than the cumulative effect of all the decisions, large and small, which have an influence on the nature of the final product. If we want to create better products and services, we need to ensure that we take the right decisions, from the beginning to the end of the project. We need a process that will take into account, as far as possible, all the factors that could affect the quality of the solution.

The quality of the solution is very largely determined, not by the **functional properties** of the product, but by the user experience associated with it. Recall from Chapter 2 that usability is one component of user experience. It is objectively measurable, as we will see in Chapter 6.

ALTERNATIVE APPROACHES TO DESIGN

User experience consultant Jared Spool (2009) has identified several different types of design decision-making that are used in the real world. We look at two of them here.

Unintended design

One commonly used style of decision-making in design is 'unintended design'. Unintended design happens when the people making decisions that affect the nature of the product do not properly consider the effect that their decisions will have. They might do this to save resources such as money or time, by doing whatever is easiest to implement. Just as frequently, they do it because they do not understand the scope or nature of the effects produced by their decision.

Usability and accessibility are particularly vulnerable to this problem: as we saw in the last chapter, software systems are often designed primarily on the basis of functional requirements, that is, what the software can do, with usability and accessibility relegated to the unimpressive-sounding category of '**non-functional**' requirements. The underlying problem is that the system boundary has been drawn too narrowly: the product's designers have focused only on the software's inherent properties, rather than taking responsibility for ensuring that the overall socio-technical system works properly. There are often commercial reasons for this: a purely product-focused approach often appears less risky and easier to control.

Self-oriented design

Sometimes an individual designer or a design team will design a product for their own purposes, in order to meet a need that they have themselves, without reference to any existing or prospective external customers. Spool (2009) calls this 'self design'. In some cases, a product designed like this may succeed in making the transition from being used exclusively by its makers to a wider circle of customers; this is unusual, however. When a product is designed in this way, its design will tend to include assumptions about the users and their needs that are not transferable outside the original environment for which it was created.

Almost all human beings have the ability to imagine themselves in someone else's situation. We are always happy to give others the benefit of the opinions we generate by doing this ('If I were you ...'). We can use this ability to draw conclusions about how something should work. What we often fail to consider is that the ability to imagine ourselves in the other person's position is not the same as sharing or understanding the other person's experience. The conclusions based on our own experience may not be applicable to others.

You are not your user!

Most people who are professionally involved in the design of software products and systems are very different in many ways from the majority of the people who are using those products and systems. For example, they may have a more sophisticated understanding of the underlying technology than the users. Therefore, as a software design professional, if you design a system that suits you, it will almost certainly *not* be suitable for most of its users.

INCLUSIVE DESIGN

Historically, a particularly common type of unwarranted assumption has been that the user will have the same set of physical and cognitive abilities as the designer. This will normally result in a design that is difficult or impossible to use for people who have various types of disability.

Fortunately, progress is being made towards a greater awareness of this problem; however, it is still common to find organisations taking an attitude towards accessibility that sees it as a box-ticking exercise. While it is true that a failure to comply with legal or regulatory accessibility requirements may expose a business to risks such as legal action, financial penalties and reputational damage, there are better arguments to be made in favour of inclusive design. Inclusive design is an approach which ensures that people with the widest possible range of abilities are explicitly taken into account during the project. This is particularly essential in the early stages. Benefits of inclusive design are listed below:

- Some of the difficulties with access that are all too familiar to people with disabilities are also encountered on an occasional basis by other users in particular circumstances. Thinking about these problems will result in a more robust and usable product.

- Users with disabilities may have goals that other users do not have. Including them at the early stages ensures that those needs will be considered before the project goes in a direction that makes it impossible.

- Users with disabilities may be engaging in the relevant activities in an environment which differs from that of other users. Again, including these users means that the design of the solution will be able to take this into account.

- If the particular needs of users with disabilities are considered at an early stage, it will often be relatively easy to include them. Retrofitting such requirements can be extremely expensive.

- Thinking carefully about how to support users with disabilities introduces an extra degree of rigour and clarity into the process, which is likely to result in a product that works better for everyone.

THE PRINCIPLES OF USER-CENTRED DESIGN

User-centred design (UCD), also known as human-centred design (HCD), avoids the problems associated with unintended design and self-oriented design (for almost any statement about UX, some practitioners can be found who disagree with it; according to one school of thought, 'human-centred' and 'user-centred' have different connotations). The international standard ISO 9241-210 (2019), 'Human-Centred Design for Interactive Systems', identifies six principles and five processes that underpin HCD/UCD. These are the central concepts in this book. We will examine each of these in turn.

Understanding users, tasks and environments

First principle of user-centred design

The design is based upon an explicit understanding of users, tasks and environments.

The most important factor in designing usable systems is understanding users and their needs. This understanding needs to be made explicit – in other words, it needs to be documented in a visible form so that project participants can share it. It will not be possible to plan a reliable and repeatable evaluation of the system's ability to meet the users' needs if they are not documented. Explicitly documenting the users' characteristics, tasks and environment helps to ensure that the design team does not forget the principle, 'you are not your user'.

It is only by taking the user's perspective that we can ensure their needs are met. Individuals vary greatly from each other and therefore, we need to ensure that we study the widest possible range of relevant potential users and environments.

A key word here is 'relevant'. An important aspect of understanding users is being clear who is not included in our user population. We must not cast the net too wide by trying to satisfy the needs of irrelevant user groups, or meet unimportant requirements.

As discussed in the last chapter, our understanding of the users and their needs can only be considered adequate if it includes an understanding of the tasks they are carrying out and the environment in which they are doing it.

Involving users

Second principle of user-centred design

Users are involved throughout design and development.

The design team needs to ensure that users are involved throughout the project. This principle should not be taken to mean that the involvement of users is required only during certain fixed periods of time that are allocated to design and development of the product in the up-front plan. On the contrary: ISO 9241-210 (2019) states, 'Human-centred design shall be planned and integrated into all phases of the product life cycle.' As mentioned earlier, the heading 'design' covers the whole project. Users must be involved for the whole duration.

It is quite common to 'involve users' in a project without really taking their participation seriously. Examples of ineffective approaches to user involvement include:

- Asking potential users what feature they would like to see in a product, without seeking empirical proof that these features would really be useful.

- Inviting users to meetings but not treating what they say as fundamentally important and acting on it.

- Giving demos or presentations to users and treating the resulting feedback as an interesting sidelight on the requirements, rather than using it to guide the project.

Effective user involvement is based on the thorough application of the first and third (see below) principles. It is not achieved through focus groups, meetings or demos. It is achieved by basing the product on an understanding of needs gained from *observing people in action*, and by evaluating successive prototypes the same way.

It is vitally important to involve the right individuals. We will see how to do this in the next chapter.

Employing user-centred evaluation to drive the design

Third principle of user-centred design

The design is driven and refined by user-centred evaluation.

One of the most significant risks on any project is that the resulting product does not successfully meet the needs of the people for whom it is intended. There is only one way of reliably making sure this does not happen: as the system evolves, have those very people try to use it in realistic ways, observe how well it performs, and use the resulting information to guide the ongoing development.

To get the most of out of using this approach, the design team will need to pay careful attention to shaping each stage of the development process so that it will result in an artefact that can be used effectively for this kind of testing, while building on the knowledge gained from previous stages.

Iterating

Fourth principle of user-centred design

The process is iterative.

User-centred design can only work if it is carried out in a series of iterations, where each iteration carries out a similar series of steps to the others. Each iteration improves upon and extends the results of the preceding ones, and must therefore be consciously designed as a learning exercise.

Iterative development is now the norm in software development (see for example Measey, 2015). It also fits in with contemporary thinking on marketing and strategy (Ries, 2011). It is a risk reduction technique, which takes into account that opportunities to gain new information are constantly arising during the development of a product. In developing iteratively, we are seeking to maximise and structure the new information as it becomes available, and to minimise the length of the feedback loop, that is, the time it takes to exploit that information by optimising the design trajectory of the product.

Addressing the whole user experience

Fifth principle of user-centred design

The design addresses the whole user experience.

User-centred design is partly concerned with ensuring the product's usability; in other words, we need to make sure that the intended users can achieve their goals effectively and efficiently. However, usability is not the only factor in achieving a good user experience. A user's experience with a product includes their emotional response to their interaction with it too.

Someone's experience of a product does not only consist of how they feel at a particular moment when they are using it, which can be referred to as *momentary* experience. There are other aspects to be considered with regard to the time dimension:

- *Anticipatory* experience refers to the user's state of mind before they start interacting with the product. They will already have feelings about the product deriving from their existing knowledge and their perception of the product's significance to them.

- *Episodic* experience refers to the user's feelings and responses as they interact with the product over a short period.

- *Cumulative* experience is the sum of the user's experience with the product up to a certain point.

At the most general level, we need to consider how using the system affects the user's life. If this is a work system, does it make their job more interesting and meaningful, or less so? Does it contribute to factors of wellbeing such as the following?

- *Mastery*: the feeling of being in control of one's environment and having an opportunity to exercise skill.

- *Autonomy*: the ability to use one's discretion and take decisions without needing to refer to others.

- *Purpose*: the sense that one's work has a meaning and is directed towards identifiable goals that one can influence.

Working in multidisciplinary teams

Sixth principle of user-centred design

The design team includes multidisciplinary skills and perspectives.

Bringing any product from an initial brief to a finished article requires a wide range of skills. The number of different individuals who are required will, of course, depend on the scope and nature of the project. It is important however that the core project personnel should be thought of as a single team. As far as possible, they should work together in one location and communicate with each other continually. The project team should not be so large as to make communication difficult, but it should be as diverse as possible, both in terms of the skills contributed by each member and also the personal characteristics and experience that each brings to bear. Roles in the team might include, but not be limited to, user researchers, interaction designers, content authors and developers.

THE USER-CENTRED DESIGN CYCLE

ISO 9241-210 (2019) identifies five areas of activity that take place in human-centred design. These are not necessarily stages to be undertaken one after the other; each of them is an ongoing process with links to the others. The processes are described below.

The design cycle is not a cookbook recipe!

It is not possible or desirable to prescribe a standard process model that can be followed step by step in every case.

The user-centred design cycle is best understood as a set of interrelated processes that take place over a period of time. There are logical dependencies between them, but this does not mean that they always have to follow one strict sequence of steps. The most important feature of the model is that it is iterative. At each iteration, the content and relative importance of the steps will differ.

Figure 3.1 shows the cycle of processes required for user-centred design. The arrows show the logical dependencies between the processes.

Another helpful way of visualising the five processes is to imagine the project as a rope or helix with five strands, as illustrated in Figure 3.2. The planning strand runs through the middle like a core. The other four strands wind around it in a spiral.

Plan the work

User-centred design cycle: process 1

Plan the human-centred design process.

Figure 3.1 The user-centred design cycle (Source: Adapted from ISO 9241-210, 2019)

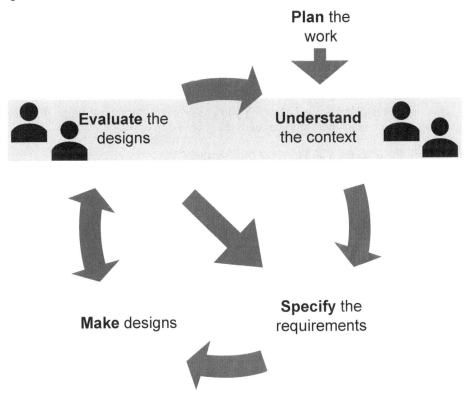

Planning is shown in Figure 3.1 as a one-off activity standing outside the main flow of the iterative sequence. In fact, planning needs to be done continually. This is a 'planning-driven' rather than 'plan-driven' approach. In other words, it is the act of planning itself that is considered valuable, rather than having activities and tasks scheduled a long way in advance and codified into a plan. 'The plans that result have a short half-life, not because they are bad plans, but because their underlying assumptions have a short half-life' (Kent Beck, quoted in Boehm and Turner, 2003).

Time spent on planning is an opportunity to configure a version of the design cycle that makes sense for the particular project or product under consideration. We need to consider:

Figure 3.2 The user-centred design helix

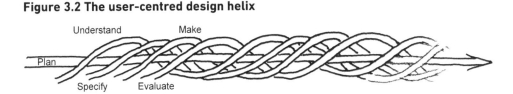

- What is the nature of the project?
- What does usability mean for this project?
- What are the types of risk that would result from poor usability?

Understanding these factors will make it possible to customise the generic UX approach for this individual project, emphasising those factors that are important and de-emphasising those that are not relevant.

Re-planning takes place at the beginning and end of every iteration through the cycle. At the beginning of each iteration the team must consider:

What are the objectives and focus of this iteration?

At the end of each iteration the team must consider:

What have we learned in this iteration, and how will we use this information in the next one?

Through this continual re-setting and re-examination of learning objectives, the team can converge on a solution that meets user needs.

Understand the context

User-centred design cycle: process 2

Understand and specify the context of use.

Planning aside, the keystone and starting point for UCD activities is user research. The objective of user research is for the design team to understand everything they need to know about the users and their characteristics, their goals, tasks and environment, in order to create a successful product or service for them.

The critical factor in user research is that it must be done by observing real users in the actual environment where they will be interacting with the system. This is indicated by the highlighted area in Figure 3.1, which shows the two processes that must be driven by user engagement.

In the early iterations, user research will be aimed at acquiring a thorough general understanding of the context, trying not to draw premature conclusions about potential solutions to specific problems. In later stages, specific areas of interest or uncertainty will be explored.

This process is discussed in Chapter 4, 'User Research'.

Specify the requirements

User-centred design cycle: process 3

Specify the user requirements.

Specifying the requirements is about first understanding users' needs, and then defining what attributes and behaviours a product or service should provide in order to meet those needs.

The specification of requirements by describing user needs and developing **user stories** is discussed in Chapter 5, 'Illustrating the Context of Use'.

Make designs

User-centred design cycle: process 4

Produce design solutions to meet user requirements.

The core activity in design is, of course, making designs. This process includes an extremely wide range of types of activity. This is not just because different projects will be aimed at producing different types of eventual product or service, it is also because each iteration in any given project will be focused on producing one or more different types of output, each of which can be considered the object of a design activity. For example, all the following are designs:

- A user journey map
- A paper-based mockup of a physical interface
- A computerised workflow simulation
- A role-playing exercise
- A hierarchy of categories for a website's navigation
- A high-fidelity interactive system prototype

There are two possible reasons for producing a design; these are not mutually exclusive, but it is important to understand which are relevant at each point. Firstly, the design may represent a set of ideas proposed for the final product or part of it. Secondly, the design may be deliberately created as an experiment, to help the design team explore issues or answer questions so as to aid progress towards the final product. Typically, designs produced in the early iterations will be mainly intended as experiments. Proposals will become more prevalent over the course of the project.

Producing design solutions is discussed further in Chapters 7–10.

Evaluate the designs

User-centred design cycle: process 5

Evaluate the designs against requirements.

Every design idea, whether embodied in a throwaway experiment or a high-fidelity prototype, needs to be evaluated. Design evaluation is the second of the two processes highlighted in Figure 3.1 as being necessarily driven by user engagement.

It would be an exaggeration to say that all design evaluation must be done by testing the design with end users. There are analytical techniques, such as heuristic evaluation, which allow alternative designs to be evaluated at the usability analyst's desk. However, even if we do this, we are still focusing on how suitable the design is for the user, rather than on any intrinsic properties of the design itself.

Evaluation is discussed in Chapter 6, 'Measuring Usability' and Chapter 11, 'Usability Evaluation'.

A note on testing

A key user experience technique is usability testing (see Chapter 11). This sometimes makes people think that UX is closely connected with user acceptance testing or system testing. While all these activities are concerned with trying to create a successful product, they have fundamentally different approaches.

Systems testing and user acceptance testing both originated as stages in a type of software quality process that is based on a full documented specification of requirements, allowing the development team to create the technical solution without reference to users (often referred to as a *waterfall* process; see Chapter 12 for more details). System testing is carried out on the finished technical solution and aims to ensure that it meets the **functional** and **non-functional requirements** specified in the documentation. User acceptance testing follows system testing, and is carried out by end users. Traditionally, this is the first opportunity that the end users have had to try using the system in a real-world situation. It is a very necessary step, because it is surprisingly easy for a solution to comply with the requirements as specified without actually meeting the users' needs.

UX, on the other hand, as described in this book, is based on user-centred design. In user-centred design, the entire process of developing a solution is driven by user-centred evaluation – in other words, if the process is carried out properly, it is not possible to end up with a solution that does not meet the users' needs. Testing becomes an iterative activity carried out over the development life cycle, and the likelihood of unpleasant surprises during final user acceptance testing is greatly diminished.

SUMMARY

Usability is part of user experience and is objectively measurable. Accessibility refers to the usability of a system by people with the widest possible range of capabilities. Inclusive design supports accessibility and usability.

User-centred design is described in the international standard ISO 9241-210 (2019), 'Human-Centred Design for Interactive Systems'. The six principles of user-centred design are:

1. The design is based upon an explicit understanding of users, tasks and environments.
2. Users are involved throughout design and development.
3. The design is driven and refined by user-centred evaluation.
4. The process is iterative.
5. The design addresses the whole user experience.
6. The design team includes multidisciplinary skills and perspectives.

The five processes of user-centred design are:

1. Plan the human-centred design process.
2. Understand and specify the context of use.
3. Specify the user requirements.
4. Produce design solutions to meet user requirements.
5. Evaluate the designs against requirements.

User experience work includes usability testing, but it is not essentially a testing discipline. Using the user-centred design approach will lead to better quality products because it focuses continually on ensuring that the product meets user needs.

REFERENCES

Beyer, H. and Holtzblatt, K. (1997) *Contextual Design: Defining Customer-Centered Systems*. Morgan Kaufmann, San Francisco, CA.

Boehm, B. and Turner, R. (2003) *Balancing Agility and Discipline: A Guide for the Perplexed*. Addison-Wesley Professional, Boston, MA.

Cadle, J. (ed.) (2014) *Developing Information Systems: Practical Guidance for IT Professionals*. BCS, Swindon.

ISO 9241-210:2019 (2019) *Ergonomics of Human-System Interaction – Part 210: Human-Centred Design for Interactive Systems*. International Organization for Standardization (ISO), Geneva.

Measey, P. (2015) *Agile Foundations: Principles, Practices and Frameworks*. BCS, Swindon.

Newman, W.M. and Lamming, M.G. (1995) *Interactive System Design*. Addison-Wesley, Reading, MA.

Ries, E. (2011) *The Lean Startup: How Today's Entrepreneurs Use Continuous Innovation to Create Radically Successful Businesses*. Penguin, London.

Shaw, G.B. (1903) *Man and Superman: A Comedy and a Philosophy*. Archibald Constable & Co, Westminster.

Spool, J. (2009) *5 Design Decision Styles. What's Yours?* Available from: https://articles.uie.com/five_design_decision_styles/

FURTHER READING

Cooper, A. (2004) *The Inmates are Running the Asylum: Why High-Tech Products Drive Us Crazy and How to Restore the Sanity*. SAMS, Indianapolis, IN.

Gould, J.D. and Lewis, C. (1985) Designing for Usability: Key Principles and What Designers Think. *Communications of the ACM*, 28(3), 300–311.

Hassell, J. (2019) *Inclusive Design for Organisations: Including your Missing 20% by Embedding Web and Mobile Accessibility*. Rethink Press, Great Yarmouth.

IEEE Standards Coordinating Committee (1990) *IEEE Standard Glossary of Software Engineering Terminology (IEEE Std 610.12-1990)*. IEEE Computer Society, Los Alamitos, CA.

Norman, D.A. (2013) *The Design of Everyday Things: Revised and Expanded Edition*. MIT Press, Cambridge, MA.

EXAMPLE EXAMINATION QUESTIONS

1. **Which of the following has the MOST significant impact on determining the usability of a system?**

   a. Creating a user interface that is visually attractive

   b. Understanding users and their needs

   c. Ensuring the design is responsive on different platforms

   d. Creating comprehensive help and documentation

2. **Which standard published by the International Organization for Standardization addresses the usability of systems?**

   a. ISO 9241

   b. ISO 9001

   c. ISO 2491

   d. ISO 1009

ANSWERS TO EXAMPLE QUESTIONS

1. The correct answer is (b).

One of the six key principles in ISO 9241-210 is 'The design is based upon an explicit understanding of users, tasks and environments'. This is summarised in answer (b). Answer (a) is an important way to improve user satisfaction with a system, but there is no point having an attractive UI if you do not understand users and their needs. (c) is a technology-based answer that will apply only to certain situations (unlike answer (a), which will always apply). Answer (d) will apply only in a situation where the system needs comprehensive help: an appropriately designed system may not need any documentation.

2. The correct answer is (a).

(a) is a multi-part standard that addresses usability and is the correct answer. (b) is incorrect because ISO 9001 is a quality standard. (c) refers to a withdrawn standard on 'Thin parallel keys and their corresponding keyways' and is nothing to do with usability. (d) refers to a standard to do with paper dimensions.

4 USER RESEARCH

When we speak of design, the real object of discussion is not the form alone, but the ensemble comprising the form and its context.

Christopher Alexander (1964)

There are known knowns; there are things we know we know. We also know there are known unknowns; that is to say, we know there are some things we do not know. But there are also unknown unknowns – the ones we don't know we don't know. And ... it is the latter category that tend to be the difficult ones.

Donald Rumsfeld (2002)

INTRODUCTION

This chapter starts by defining a central concept in human-centred design: the **context of use.** We then move on to discuss how this can be studied and understood through user research. We look at the main types of *subjective* or opinion-based research, which is about listening to users' opinions, before explaining why *empirical*, behaviour-based research, based on studying evidence, is a more reliable basis for design. The key method described is **contextual inquiry**. We investigate how to do this using field visits.

LEARNING OBJECTIVES

After reading this chapter you will be able to:

Remember	• State the components of the context of use
	• State the difference between observation and interpretation
	• List discount usability research techniques that can be used to develop a shared knowledge of the context of use, such as diary studies
	• State the key principles of contextual inquiry
	• Define affinity diagramming
	• Recognise that requirements gathering and conceptual design should be truly inclusive
Understand	• Identify the potential users of the system
	• Recognise good and poor questions to ask in user interviews
	• Describe the kinds of data that should be collected during a site visit to users

Apply	• Plan site visits to end users to understand the context of use
	• Choose the appropriate research method to understand the context of use
	• Demonstrate the difference between opinion-based and behaviour-based research methods
	• Interpret the data from a site visit in ways that can be used to understand the context of use

THE ROLE OF USER RESEARCH

Imagine that you have what you think is a great idea for a product. Should you immediately go out and invest your savings, or borrow money, to bring your idea to market? You would probably want to think about it first. You might prefer to start by getting some information, so that your eventual decision would be based on something better than a hunch. How should you go about finding out whether people would buy your product? You could ask them. But exactly who do we mean by 'them'? And what should you ask them? Just as importantly, how will you satisfy yourself that the answers they give you are an accurate prediction of their future actions? Then again, perhaps you should start by deciding exactly what features and functionality your product will provide ...

These are some of the questions that we can start to address by carrying out user research. User research is the only way of laying a firm foundation to support our product design. Our first objective will be to understand the **context of use**.

UNDERSTANDING THE CONTEXT OF USE

The best design will be the one that best fits the context of use for the product being developed. In describing the context of use, we are defining the parameters that constrain the design of the product. The most important aspects of the context of use are the people who will be using the product, and the tasks that they will be performing in using it. However, we also need to understand the other elements of the physical and social environment, besides the product that we are designing, and the other resources available to the users that play a role. This includes any other tools that are being used.

Definition: the context of use

The users, goals and tasks, resources, and the technical, physical, social, cultural and organisational environments in which a product is used (ISO 9241-11, 2018)

Figure 4.1 illustrates some of the components of the context of use that are identified in ISO 9241-11. As the diagram shows, there are a large number of aspects to take into consideration.

Figure 4.1 Components of the context of use (Source: Based on ISO 9241-11)

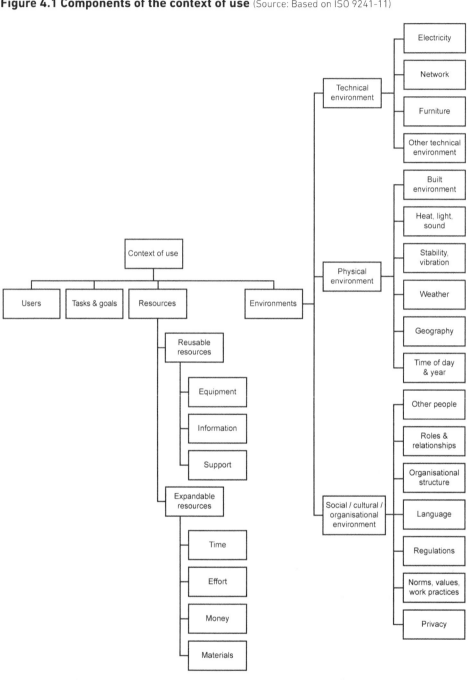

PACT

A mnemonic sometimes used for remembering the elements of the context of use is 'PACT': people, activities, contexts, technologies. The 'contexts' referred to here are what ISO 9241-11 (2018) calls 'environments', the other equivalent terms are shown below (both the elements and terms may be used in the Foundation Certificate examination).

PACT element	Equivalent term in ISO 9241-11
People	Users
Activities	Tasks and goals
'Contexts'	Physical and social environments
Technologies	Resources, technical environment

IDENTIFYING WHICH PEOPLE TO STUDY

As we saw in the last chapter, user research is about observing real users in their real environment. That is easy to articulate as a general principle, but if we are to come up with an actionable research plan, we must identify exactly which individuals we are going to study, where and how.

What makes some people more suitable objects of study than others? The answer is given by looking at the other three components of the context of use: tasks, resources and environment. We are designing a product or service for people carrying out particular tasks in certain environments. Therefore, what we need to look for is people who are carrying out the same tasks – or seeking the same goals – in the same environments, using (where applicable) the same equipment and other resources. If we are designing specifically for a population with certain predispositions or physical attributes, then we will need to take that into account as well; but most often we will be trying to cater for the widest possible range of individuals.

Ideally, we will find an exact match between our study participants and all the context-of-use elements. If we are designing a mobile phone application to help children stay safe when travelling to school by bus in outer London, for example, we will need to look for the elements shown in Table 4.1

Table 4.1 Examples of context-of-use elements

Context-of-use element	Details
Users	Schoolchildren (a particular age group?)
Tasks and goals	Travel to school, keep safe
Environments	Bus in outer London at school time, alone or in a group
Resources	Mobile phone, internet connectivity, battery power

In this example, there should be no difficulty in finding a good supply of research participants. Examples of the environment are easily accessed and there are large numbers of people meeting the criteria. It would not be appropriate to compromise on any of them – for example, by studying adults going to work, or by studying schoolchildren in rural Lincolnshire.

Even where the context of use is less easily accessed, it is crucial that we find a good match between all the elements. Our research findings will be much less valuable, or even completely misleading, if we do not look at people who have the relevant goals and who are in the right environments. Finding the right people can be difficult, and sometimes we meet with pressure from business stakeholders to compromise. Suppose that we are designing a system to help firefighters communicate with their control room while driving to an emergency. There might be a temptation to ask how we can study people in that environment. Could we study firefighters when they are not travelling to an emergency? Or: we are already doing some work for an ambulance service – would it be easier to study paramedics when they are travelling to an emergency instead? But this is not acceptable – any kind of compromise on the criteria will potentially lead to invalid conclusions.

When a business is designing for their existing customers, they might think that they already know a great deal about them, so there is no need to go out and study their customers. It may very well be true that people in the organisation have a lot of knowledge about their customers, and we should make the best possible use of that insight. However, knowledge about customers gained from people in the business can never be a substitute for carrying out user research.

If it is genuinely impossible to get access to the users in the correct environment, which may be the case with people who work in highly stressful or dangerous environments, then there is no alternative but to study them in some other circumstances. This might call for some ingenuity. A good opportunity might present itself when they are carrying out related tasks in a different environment, for example when they are undertaking training. The most essential requirement is to study the right people.

We need a supply of individuals that we can turn to throughout the life of our project. Bear in mind that once individuals have taken part in a certain amount of testing, they will accumulate knowledge about the design, which may make them less suitable participants in some activities.

Inclusive research

As we have seen, choosing research participants is above all a matter of restricting the type of people we study to fit the context of use. However, once those restrictions are taken into account, we also need to make sure that the people we study are representative of the widest possible range of prospective users. This means making a conscious effort to study people with a variety of physical, cognitive and personality characteristics.

TYPES OF USER RESEARCH

This section will look at some specific techniques for studying the context of use. We can identify several different dimensions for categorising the techniques.

Quantitative versus qualitative research

The purpose of our research is to help us make decisions. Particularly when comparing alternatives, it can be very helpful to have findings that are expressed in terms of numbers. **Quantitative** research allows us to make comparisons more easily. **Qualitative** research findings, by contrast, describe the subject matter in a more diffuse way that may be equally valid, but is not framed numerically.

Sometimes people think that quantitative findings are the more 'scientific'. They are certainly more in tune with traditional 20th-century management styles and therefore can be more persuasive with managers. However, both types of result are valuable. Qualitative findings help us to make sense of our quantitative findings and provide a richer understanding of the context of use. Quantitative findings provide focus and help us to identify the way forwards.

> Very often we will be using research methods that result in a lot of unstructured information, such as interview transcripts. With careful analysis, however, we can derive quantitative measures from the mass of detail.

It is important not to misuse numbers by trying to carry out inappropriate arithmetic operations. It is valid to calculate the average amount of time that people spend on a given task using interface A, and compare this to the average calculated for interface B, for example, drawing the conclusion that interface B is 20 per cent faster. On the other hand, it is not valid to assess people's satisfaction with the two interfaces on a scale from 1 to 5 and draw the conclusion that A is 30 per cent more satisfactory. This is because the scale being used in the first case is genuinely zero-based (time elapsed), whereas the scale in the second case is based on arbitrary numbers that cannot yield an average or ratio.

Subjective versus empirical research

In our normal human interactions, we tend to feel that our understanding of people comes from communicating with them. We would not think that we necessarily understood a person very well simply from observing what they did over a limited period. In user research, though, we cannot rely only on talking to people. We need our information to be as accurate, complete and reliable as possible; one of the worst possible ways of getting this kind of information about a person is to ask them to give it to you. There are several reasons for this:

- People are not very good at seeing themselves objectively or predicting their own future actions in a hypothetical scenario.

- People often do not remember the details of an experience accurately; they can be unaware of this and it does not stop them from unconsciously constructing a version of events that seems coherent and appropriate – and therefore true – to them.

- Providing someone with information that they have asked for is an example of social interaction. Social interactions are strongly influenced by a host of subtle and often unconscious factors on the part of those involved, such as their attitude towards the other party, their wish to project a certain image of themselves, or their sense of an obligation to protect the other's feelings by giving the desired answers.

- Whereas design professionals are used to envisioning products and systems that do not currently exist, and imagining users' reactions to them, this is not part of everyone's everyday experience.

Of course, we do need to ask people questions and pay attention to their answers, but we need to be aware that the information we get this way is *subjective* or opinion-based. It has been passed through many cognitive and social filters before it reaches us. We need to supplement it with information that we find out for ourselves, which has not been through those filters and is consequently more reliable – in other words, *empirical* or behaviour-based information.

Face-to-face versus remote research

We need to examine the context of use directly. Ideally, we would always be physically present in the environment under study; *face-to-face* research gives access to a wide range of information that would otherwise be hidden from us. Real-world projects require us to work within constraints, however. For example, there may not be enough time to carry out as much research as we would like, or perhaps the people we need to study are distributed in different geographical locations that make it impossible to visit them all. Advances in technology now make it easier to do some user research *remotely*.

Moderated versus unmoderated research

Whether the researcher is present with the people being studied or not, they may choose to direct the session in a structured way (moderated research), to ensure focus on getting answers to comparatively clear and specific research questions that are known in advance; or they may allow the session to unfold in a less predictable manner (unmoderated research). This is a good approach when looking for 'unknown unknowns'.

OPINION-BASED RESEARCH

How should we go about studying people? How can we find out what they want? One possible answer to this is, of course, to ask them what they want. Commonly used tools for asking people what they want include surveys, focus groups and interviews.

Surveys and questionnaires

For our purposes, a survey and a questionnaire are different words for the same thing: a set of questions in written form that we might ask orally but more commonly are given to participants for them to fill in the answers in writing – traditionally on paper, but nowadays almost always online. The set of questions is standardised, so that we can analyse the answers from a large set of respondents using arithmetical and statistical methods. For this to work, we must be as sure as reasonably possible that every participant understands the questions in the same way, and that the differences between the answers they give accurately represent the differences in their opinions. The questions must therefore be clear and unambiguous. Preferably, they need to be 'closed' questions – in other words, it must be possible to present a list of options for each question for the respondent to choose from. The options presented must follow the MECE rule. This stands for 'mutually exclusive and collectively exhaustive', and refers to the requirement that there should be exactly one selectable option for any one valid response to a given question.

The strong point of surveys is that they can be used to get responses from a large number of people. However, when doing user research, this advantage is often outweighed by the disadvantages, which are chiefly:

- The clarity required on questions and possible answers when setting up a questionnaire may not be appropriate or even possible when starting a design project. In such situations, not only do we not know the answers to the questions, but we do not even know what the right questions to ask are – hence the quotation from Donald Rumsfeld at the beginning of this chapter.

- Particularly when administered in the most efficient way, that is, using web forms, surveys preclude the gathering of any information at all other than the answers to the questions that are asked. By their very nature, they do not give any opportunity to understand and evaluate the participants' environments. This is crucial information.

Generally speaking, then, surveys and questionnaires are not useful tools when carrying out user research in a people-oriented design process. That is not to say there are never situations where they can be helpful, but these are the exception rather than the rule.

Focus groups

A focus group is a group of people, previously unknown to each other, who have been brought together to have a discussion on a specific set of topics. The term 'focus group' is commonly used to refer to the session itself where the discussion takes place. Like surveys, focus groups have been used in marketing for several decades. The technique is designed to capture people's opinions, attitudes and preferences in relation to a subject, and to gather information about the process whereby an individual may form their opinion on that subject, particularly the way in which opinions are developed in conversation with others.

Focus group discussions can sometimes be illuminating, but they are an inherently artificial environment, and are prone to manipulation and distortion by individuals within the group. Information gained from them is not necessarily a reliable reflection of what people really think and do in the normal course of their lives.

Interviews

The word 'interview' brings up many associations in peoples' minds – they think of job recruitment interviews, television news interviews and so on. For our purposes, though, an interview is simply an opportunity to spend some time talking to a potential user of our product, in order to find out how and what they think about the subject area. An interview might be carried out in the user's workplace, in your office or in a neutral venue. A standalone interview typically lasts between 30 minutes and an hour.

Interviews provide unrivalled possibilities for understanding users and finding out new ways of thinking about a problem. The information that we gain from an interview is necessarily subjective, because what the interviewee tells us will reflect their own personal thoughts, feelings, opinions and preferences; ultimately, they will say what they feel like saying. However, skilful interviewing will help to maximise the accuracy and completeness of what the interviewee tells us. Another layer of subjectivity is involved when we record and interpret what was said: in this case, it is our own prejudices and worldview that we need to try to factor out.

Because we have almost all been talking to other people for our whole lives, there is a temptation to think that interviewing is easy. In fact, it is a very hard skill to master. We need to unlearn some of the habits that we have developed in normal social settings. For example, we often spend much of a conversation talking about ourselves, or looking for an opportunity to get across our own view on the subject matter, or thinking about what to say next, or about how to turn the conversation in a particular direction. We aim to generate support from, or develop rapport with someone by asking leading questions, 'putting words in their mouth' and generally encouraging them to agree with our point of view. All these tendencies are unhelpful in user research interviewing, which requires complete sublimation of our own viewpoint, openness to whatever the interviewee might say, and commitment to listening and understanding. At all costs we need to avoid 'leading questions', that is, questions that orientate the interviewee towards a particular answer, such as 'Do you think ...?', 'Don't you sometimes ...?', 'Would you say that ...?' or 'Isn't it annoying that ...?'

We can increase the reliability of the information gained from interviews by paying very close attention to the words we use, so that we know whether we are asking for facts or opinions. Similarly, we need to analyse what is being said, to assess the level of subjectivity. We may be interested in feelings and opinions, but it is more useful to gather objective facts about goals, tasks, activities, tools, interactions, pain points and workarounds. This can be achieved by sticking to descriptions of past events, which we can elicit by asking **recall questions** like 'When was the last time you ...?', or 'How many times in the last week have you ...?' It is less useful to ask what people intend to do in the future, or what they might do in a hypothetical situation – this information is unverifiable and may be completely wrong.

One key issue is the degree to which the interview should be planned and directed. This partly depends on what stage of the project has been reached. In the early stages, it is best to let the interviewee dictate the content and direction of the conversation.

Here, the researcher is not looking for answers to specific 'known unknowns', but trying to minimise the number of 'unknown unknowns'. Later, as the team starts to develop alternative hypotheses about the best way forward, the scope of questions will narrow.

Experienced IT professionals sometimes find it hard to get themselves into the right mindset for user research interviewing. This is not about analytically determining the gaps in one's knowledge on points of detail and seeking information to fill those gaps; nor is it about trying to define a problem solution. It is about acting in a way that is most likely to lead the interviewee to reveal new insights into their own motivations, behaviours and thought processes. A large part of this is creating an atmosphere of partnership. It is vitally important that the interviewee should not see the researcher as an expert who has all the answers or who is testing them in some way. For this reason, it is helpful to 'dress down', avoid talking about oneself and show humility rather than trying to impress. This may sometimes include feigning ignorance of things we do already know.

Empathy

User researchers sometimes refer to seeking 'empathy' with users. This is not a synonym for rapport. It does not denote a subjective state of mind on the part of the researcher, still less a way of emotionally interrelating with users – it simply refers to developing a deep and detailed understanding of people's lived experience, in so far as it relates to the project in hand.

Some people have been trained to use 'active listening', which involves the interviewer paraphrasing in their own terms what the interviewee has just said. While it is good to reflect back what has been said, it is inadvisable to use our own words to do it. If we introduce extraneous concepts and terminology, we are shifting the conversation onto our own ground rather than remaining in the interviewees' territory, which is where we should aim to stay.

A checklist of question types

User research consultant Steve Portigal (2013) offers a useful taxonomy of interview question types:

Questions that gather context and collect details:

- Ask about organisational structure
- Ask about relationships
- Ask about task sequence
- Ask about quantities

- Ask for examples
- Ask about exceptions
- Ask for complete lists

Questions that probe what's been unsaid:

- Ask for clarification
- Ask for explanations of local or specialist words
- Follow up emotional cues
- Ask why
- Probe delicately
- Probe without presuming
- Ask how to explain to an outsider
- Ask how to teach another person

Questions that create contrasts so as to uncover frameworks and mental models:

- Compare processes
- Compare with others
- Compare across time

BEHAVIOUR-BASED RESEARCH

We have seen how we cannot necessarily put much faith in the information we get when we ask people what they want. It is more reliable to observe what people actually do. A highly effective way of doing this is by carrying out **contextual inquiry**, or field visits, to study people in the relevant environment, whether that is their workplace, their home or some other place where they engage in the relevant activity.

Contextual inquiry

The terms 'contextual inquiry' and 'ethnography' are used largely interchangeably. They both refer to an approach that involves studying a few individuals in depth by carrying out field visits to achieve a deep understanding of their activities and goals, the way they interact with technology and with other people and the difficulties they encounter. Studying a few individuals in this way allows a clearer focus on the needs that people have in common, and also the ways in which needs differ between different groups.

Suggested key steps to follow when conducting a field visit are summarised graphically in Figure 4.2 and are as follows:

Figure 4.2 Key steps in conducting a field visit

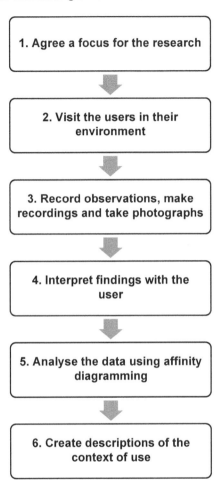

Agree a focus for the research
The biggest challenge with a field visit is the sheer volume of information that is available. Without a clear idea of what you want to achieve, it is all too easy to come back to the office without being entirely sure what has been learned. Involve the rest of your team in a quick brainstorm of questions they would like the answers to, arrange the questions into groups, and choose the most important group as the 'focus question' for your visit.

Visit the users in their environment
You may be visiting one individual or several individuals at the same organisation. The visit could take anything between two hours or two days – potentially even longer. The session with each participant will start with a short interview so that you can explain the purpose of the visit and the method you will be using. It is vitally important that the participants understand that you want to see and hear them carrying out their normal tasks in the normal way. If you arrive for a contextual inquiry visit and find that a meeting room has been booked for the duration, you will have some explaining to do.

Two is a good number of researchers to take on a field visit. If there is only one, you may miss information. If there are three or more, there is a risk of swamping the participants and introducing aspects of your own working culture into the situation, instead of being attuned to the participants' culture.

It is important to ask the participants for permission to take notes, take photographs, make audio recordings or make video recordings before you do so. Explain why this is being done, tell them that they are entitled to withdraw their permission for you to do so at any time, and make a commitment to keeping these materials within the team and destroying them when possible. It is good practice to ask the participants to sign a form acknowledging that they understand this and have given their permission. At the same time, try not to introduce too much formality into the situation. The participants need to understand that they are not being assessed in any way.

Informed consent

When conducting any kind of user research, we need to treat the participants with respect. This means putting their interests first and ensuring they feel in control of the process. We must seek their permission for what we are doing and ensure that it is given on the basis of a clear and accurate understanding. In particular we need to:

- Tell the participants what we are going to do.
- Explain what we want them to do.
- Explain the purpose of the research activity.
- Explain how we are going to use the material collected, including:
  - Whether we are going to share it with anyone.
  - If so, with whom and why.
  - How long we are going to keep it.
- Ensure they understand that they can withdraw at any time.

Record observations, make recordings and take photographs

Once the introductory interview is out of the way and participant consent has been given, it is a matter of being as unobtrusive as possible, while asking about everything that needs explaining. Make notes of any observations that seem as if they might be significant, but avoid trying to write everything down. Your focus needs to be on the participants rather than your notepad.

It is essential to make an audio recording of the session. No one can take notes covering everything during a session, and the participants are likely to say some things whose significance only becomes apparent later. The transcript of the recording will be a central document in the subsequent analysis.

Observations

In this book, when we talk about an **observation**, we mean *something that you see or hear* on a field visit: an incontrovertible objective finding. This is distinct from something that you infer from what has been seen or heard – that is an **interpretation**. Observations are the 'gold dust' or nuggets of goodness that we are looking for on a field visit.

This is also distinct from the use of the word 'observation' to refer to the general technique of eliciting information by watching and listening to users as they go about their business.

Some researchers like to make video recordings as well as audio recordings. The main danger with this is that the participants will feel more self-conscious being filmed, and therefore may not behave naturally. It is only in a small subset of environments that video adds important additional information that audio does not capture. However, it is often useful to take photographs, either of a specific tool being used or of the general environment. These will help the other members of your team to picture the scene. Don't make a fuss about it, or use any special equipment – just take a quick snap.

Two other sets of information you may want to keep for future reference are:

- A glossary of technical terms and abbreviations with their meanings
- A list of the participants that you have worked with

AEIOU

A useful mnemonic for remembering what to write down is AEIOU – activities, environments, interactions, objects and users.

Activities: What do the participants do? How do they talk about what they do? Which are the tasks that are most important in achieving their goals?

Environments: Record everything about the physical and social environment that will help to give your colleagues the full picture.

Interactions: Who does the participant need to speak with, send a message to or receive a message from in order to carry out their tasks? What communications systems (high or low tech) do they interact with? Where does communication seem to break down?

Objects: What physical objects play a part in the user's activities? In particular, are there any that act as 'boundary objects', conveying information from one person or group to another?

Users: What can you say about the users that will be useful for design, or that will help you later to find other people with similar attributes? What are their motivations? What experience and skills do they have?

Interpret findings with the user

Our observations during a field visit are particularly valuable because they are empirical data. However, the real meaning of what we have observed may not be apparent to us. We might notice that the user is taking what seems to be a roundabout approach to carrying out a task, or introducing steps into the process whose value is not immediately apparent. This is why we need to carry out this fourth step while we are still in the user's environment, and check our understanding or ask for clarification of anything that might possibly be open to alternative interpretations, even if we think we understand it.

Analyse the data using affinity diagramming

The data that we collect from a field visit is qualitative and rather unstructured. We are faced with two questions at this point. First, how can we analyse this data in a rigorous way while still maintaining an authentic focus on the participants' experience? Second, how can we merge our findings from multiple contextual sessions into one coherent body of research output?

There are two ways of doing this. One aims to squeeze every ounce of value out of the field visit documents and maximise the rigour achieved, but is comparatively time-consuming and expensive. This involves getting transcripts of the sessions, then going through the transcripts, carefully listing everything that can be found under each of the AEIOU headings. Also list what each participant has revealed about their opinions, beliefs and preferences, but keep these opinion-based findings clearly distinguished from the objective description of the context of use. Each finding needs to be recorded as an independent item in the list. All these items can then be checked against the photographs and notes from the session. This comparatively formal approach is suitable for projects where the team is only going to have the opportunity to do one round of field visits.

The alternative method, which will probably deliver 80 per cent of the benefit, is very much faster and yields information that can be used almost immediately by the rest of the team. In this approach, we simply take the observations recorded in our notes during the session and write each one on a sticky note. These can then be placed on a wall and organised into related groups. This is known as affinity diagramming (Figure 4.3). If we have findings from more than one session, we can merge the sticky notes from all the sessions at this point. Clearly, this method puts a greater responsibility on the researcher to take good notes during the session, as there is no transcript to work from later, but it is recommended for projects where there are plenty of opportunities for field visits.

Create descriptions of the context of use

Having itemised all our findings and organised them into groups, we can then proceed to create some design artefacts that make the information easily digestible for our colleagues. One good technique for this is the empathy map format (Osterwalder and Pigneur, 2010), like the one in Figure 4.4. This is a simple template that allows us to record:

- What the user *thinks and feels* – what really matters to them?
- What the user *hears* in their physical and social surroundings
- What the user *sees*
- What the user *says* and *does*
- The user's *pains and gains* – the aspects or stages of the experience that make it more or less painful or easy for them

Figure 4.3 Affinity diagram

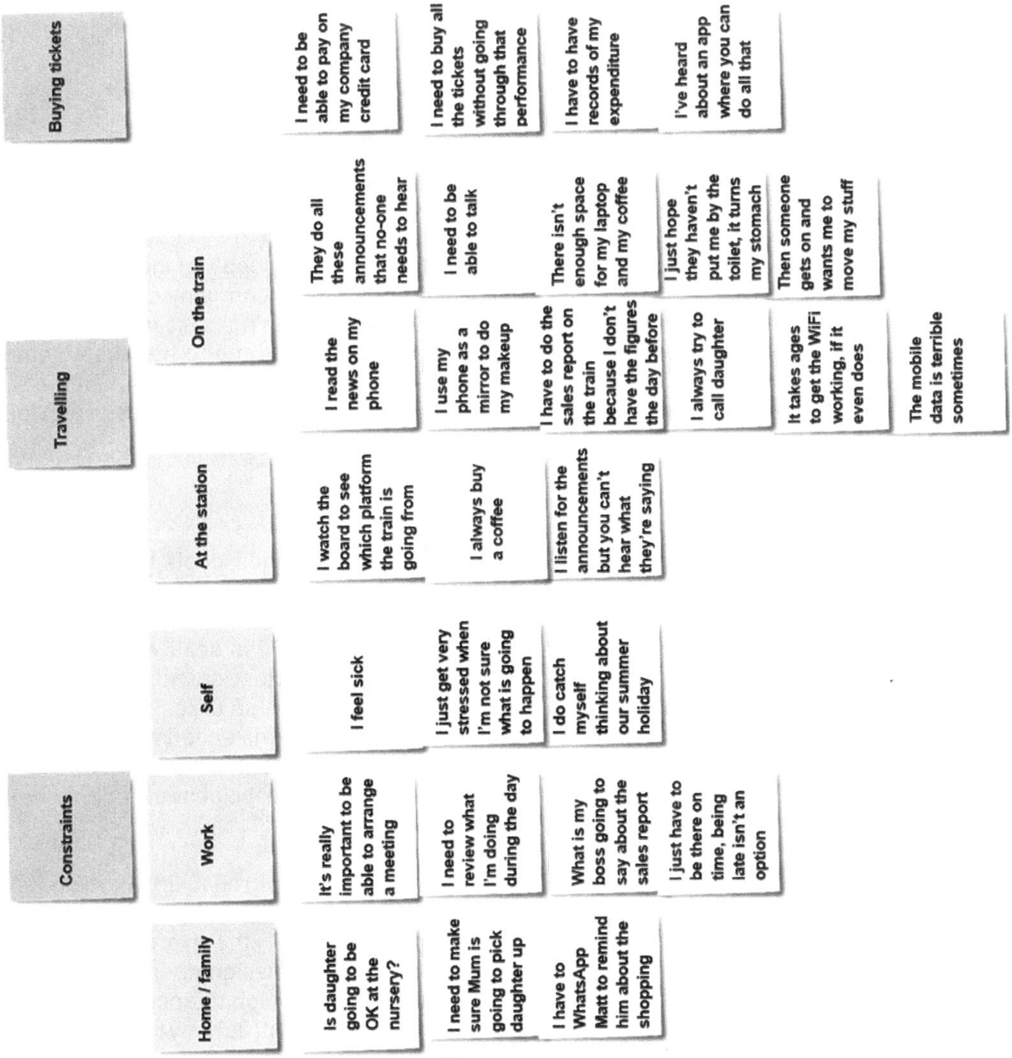

Constraints

Travelling

Buying tickets

Home / family	Work	Self	At the station	On the train	Buying tickets
Is daughter going to be OK at the nursery?	It's really important to be able to arrange a meeting	I feel sick	I watch the board to see which platform the train is going from	They do all these announcements that no-one needs to hear	I need to be able to pay on my company credit card
I need to make sure Mum is going to pick daughter up	I need to review what I'm doing during the day	I just get very stressed when I'm not sure what is going to happen	I always buy a coffee	I read the news on my phone	I need to be able to talk	I need to buy all the tickets without going through that performance
I have to WhatsApp Matt to remind him about the shopping	What is my boss going to say about the sales report	I do catch myself thinking about our summer holiday	I listen for the announcements but you can't hear what they're saying	I use my phone as a mirror to do my makeup	There isn't enough space for my laptop and my coffee	I have to have records of my expenditure
	I just have to be there on time, being late isn't an option			I have to do the sales report on the train because I don't have the figures the day before	I just hope they haven't put me by the toilet, it turns my stomach	I've heard about an app where you can do all that
				I always try to call daughter	Then someone gets on and wants me to move my stuff	
				It takes ages to get the WiFi working, if it even does		
				The mobile data is terrible sometimes		

We can create an empathy map by simply drawing the template on a whiteboard or large sheet of paper and then putting the sticky notes on it, or by using software. Electronic documents have many advantages, such as reliable permanent storage and the ability to be copied, edited and reproduced. However, using sticky notes is quicker and makes the team feel more directly in touch with the original research, and hence the users.

We will look at other techniques for describing the context of use, such as personas and journey maps, in the next chapter.

DISCOUNT TECHNIQUES

Contextual inquiry is a comparatively expensive technique, taking into account the logistics, preparation and analysis. There are some other techniques that require either less preparation or fewer resources, and hence are sometimes collectively referred to as **discount techniques**.

Popup interviews

At some point in your project it is likely that some questions will arise which can only be answered reliably by doing some user research, but there are no field visits planned, and you need an answer quickly. This situation can be dealt with by conducting *popup interviews*. Identify a place where you are likely to find a good supply of individuals who fit the profile of your expected user base. This might be the company canteen, if the system is an in-house business application, or a coffee shop in the case of a consumer system. Go there and ask people for a few minutes of their time to ask them some questions. A surprising number of people will generally be willing to help. An interview like this does not give you the ability to study the users' environment, but it does provide an opportunity to ask them about their goals and tasks.

Diary studies

On some projects, you may want to study a good sample of individuals to understand a task or small set of tasks that do not occur at predictable times or take up a large proportion of the individuals' time. For example, you might want to know how often a task or issue occurs, how long it takes to deal with it, how it is dealt with and what problems occur in the process. It is not economically practicable to spend hours or days visiting people and waiting for the right thing to happen. In these cases, a **diary study** can help. Here, the researcher delegates the job of recording the situation to the users themselves. This might be done with a paper form, an online form or a mobile app. The researcher asks the participant to record certain details of the incident every time that it occurs.

The main drawback with diary studies is the findings' lack of reliability. Participants may not follow the instructions correctly and invent information for the sake of having something to report. Alternatively, they may lose interest in the exercise and stop recording anything after a while. This can be addressed by designing incentives that encourage the participants to persevere with the exercise. Mobile apps can provide periodic reminders, although this needs to be done in a non-intrusive way.

Figure 4.4 Empathy map

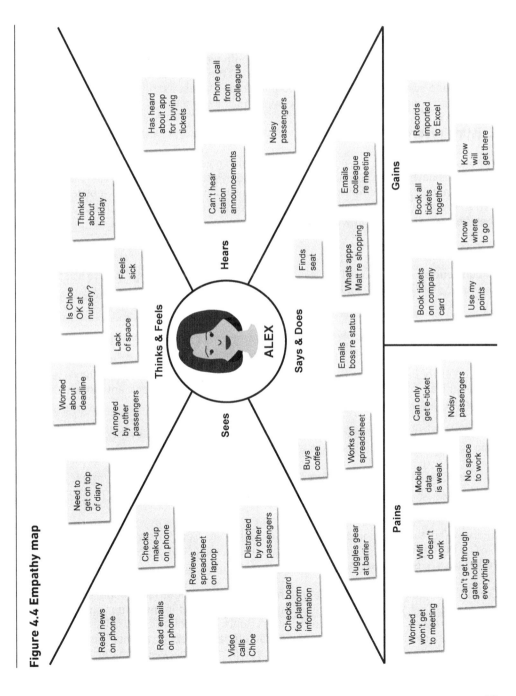

53

Remote desktop access

Often, some of the users that we would like to study are located somewhere that is hard to get to, such as another country. If it is not possible to arrange a visit, one way of understanding at least those parts of their work that are done using a computer is to arrange a screen sharing session. This can be done using web meeting software. If the user shares their screen with you, you can watch and ask questions using the audio connection while the user goes about their work. One advantage of using this method is that you can record the session, including both video and audio, and replay it later to study interesting sections. Of course, there is little opportunity to find out about the physical and social environment, although you can at least ask the participant to show you the surroundings using their webcam, if they have one.

Existing records

Various types of records are often available which give an insight into interactions that customers have with a company and its services. For example, *web server logs* can be an excellent source of empirical data on the way in which people use a website. Typical paths through the site's navigation structure or transactional logic can be identified, together with the points at which users decide to leave the site.

Call centres use systems that record customer service calls. These can be a useful source of insight into customers' experience.

SUMMARY

The context of use includes the users, their goals and tasks, the resources they use and the technical, physical, social, cultural and organisational environments in which the system is used.

The 'users' that we will need to study are the people with the relevant characteristics who are pursuing relevant goals in relevant environments.

Empirical, behaviour-based research methods, such as contextual inquiry, make a more reliable basis for design than subjective, opinion-based methods such as questionnaires or focus groups.

Interviewing, though subjective, is a useful technique. Good interview questions avoid biasing the participant towards a particular answer and ask about recent historical facts rather than hypothetical future situations.

Contextual inquiry is an empirical method that gives insight into people's goals and environment by studying a limited number of individuals in depth during site visits. The researcher collects data about activities, tools, pain points and workarounds. This information is recorded as a large set of discrete factual observations. These are then interpreted with the user to generate understanding and analysed with the design team using affinity diagramming to identify common issues and ideas about problem areas. The information can be presented in an empathy map to help the team develop an understanding of the users.

Site visits can be supplemented by discount usability techniques such as popup interviews and diary studies.

REFERENCES

Alexander, C. (1964) *Notes on the Synthesis of Form*. Harvard University Press, Cambridge, MA.

ISO 9241-11:2018 (2018) *Ergonomics of Human-System Interaction – Part 11: Usability: Definitions and Concepts*. International Organization for Standardization (ISO), Geneva.

Osterwalder, A. and Pigneur, Y. (2010) *Business Model Generation: A Handbook for Visionaries, Game Changers, and Challengers*. John Wiley & Sons, Hoboken, NJ.

Portigal, S. (2013) *Interviewing Users*. Rosenfeld Media, Brooklyn, NY.

Rumsfeld, D. (2002) U.S. Department of Defense: News Transcript: DoD News Briefing – Secretary Rumsfeld and Gen. Myers. Available from: https://archive.defense.gov/Transcripts/Transcript.aspx?TranscriptID=2636

FURTHER READING

Beyer, H. and Holtzblatt, K. (1997) *Contextual Design: Defining Customer-Centered Systems*. Morgan Kaufmann, San Francisco, CA.

Fitzpatrick, R. (2013) *The Mom Test: How to Talk to Customers and Learn If Your Business is a Good Idea when Everyone is Lying to You*. CreateSpace Independent Publishing Platform, Scotts Valley, CA.

Goodman, E., Kuniavsky, M. and Mode, A. (2012) *Observing the User Experience: A Practitioner's Guide to User Research*. Morgan Kaufmann, San Francisco, CA.

Goodwin, K. (2011) *Designing for the Digital Age: How to Create Human-Centered Products and Services*. Wiley, Indianapolis, IN.

Marsh, S. (2018) *User Research*. Kogan Page, London.

Travis, D. and Hodgson, P. (2019) *Think like a UX Researcher: How to Observe Users, Influence Design, and Shape Business Strategy*. Taylor & Francis, Boca Raton, FL.

EXAMPLE EXAMINATION QUESTIONS

1. The designers of a new in-flight entertainment system to be used on an aeroplane want to test out the user interface. Who would you recommend they recruit for a usability test?

   a. Ground staff at airports who speak with customers every day

   b. People who own an interactive digital television in their home

   c. People who have travelled on two or more long-haul flights in the last 6 months

   d. Regular movie-goers who have been to the cinema at least once a month over the last year

2. When trying to understand user requirements, why is it unsuitable to simply ask people what they want?

   a. Any designs resulting from these interviews will lack originality

   b. User requirements need to be based on organisational goals

   c. People do not have good insight into their needs from a system

   d. User interviews are too complex to analyse in any meaningful way

3. A design team in the early stages of the design of an in-store shopping basket with a digital interface has approached you to carry our user research. They suggest you interview 10 of their internal staff who regularly shop in supermarkets. How should you respond?

   a. 10 users is too few to collect adequate data

   b. It would be better to observe staff as they shop

   c. It would be more cost-effective to run a focus group than separate interviews

   d. Any research should be carried out with real users, not internal staff

4. What are the components of the context of use?

   a. Users, UX vision and testing

   b. Users, environments and tasks

   c. Users, personas and key performance indicators (KPIs)

   d. Users, prototyping and testing

ANSWERS TO EXAMPLE QUESTIONS

1. The correct answer is (c).

The purpose behind this question is to check that candidates are aware that they should run tests with real users of the system, not people who are similar to real users or that speak for users. (a) is the wrong choice because ground staff are not users of the system. (b) is the wrong choice because the context of using an interactive television in the home is very different from using a system on an aeroplane. (d) is the wrong choice because movie-goers are not necessarily airline travellers. This leaves (c) as the best choice since this group will contain the actual users of the system.

2. The correct answer is (c).

This question tests a candidate's knowledge of this classic user research issue: it's not what users say, it's what users do that matters. (d) is wrong, because the qualitative data from user interviews can be analysed with many techniques, including affinity mapping. (b) is wrong: organisational goals are important but they do not trump user goals. (a) is wrong because originality isn't the issue here; and anyway, users may still come up with original ideas that do not meet their needs.

3. The correct answer is (d).

The aim of this question is to ensure candidates understand that the most important people to observe during a field visit are the intended users of the system. Option (a) is a red herring, since as few as five people will still provide some insights. (b) is a better choice as it captures context, but it still omits the actual users of the system. (c) is a poor choice since it ignores both the user's context and the users themselves. This leaves (d) as the correct answer.

4. The correct answer is (b).

(b) is the correct answer because ISO 9241-11 describes the context of use as comprising a description of users, tasks, environments and equipment. (a), (c) and (d) all correctly contain 'users', but also have distracter buzzwords, none of which relates to environments or tasks.

5 ILLUSTRATING THE CONTEXT OF USE

> Perfection is finally attained not when there is no longer anything to add, but when there is no longer anything to take away.
>
> Antoine de Saint-Exupéry (1939)

INTRODUCTION

This chapter describes how to document our understanding of the context of use in a way that will help the team to take the design forward. We start by reviewing the elements of the context of use that should be documented. We then explore a handful of key techniques for doing this, including the use of personas, user journey maps and scenarios. We introduce the concept of **user needs**. We consider the importance of keeping the interface simple, as shown by **Hick's law**, and note how defining *key tasks* can help us do this. Finally, we describe **user stories**, a developer-friendly format for defining what the system should do.

LEARNING OBJECTIVES

After reading this chapter you will be able to:

Remember	• State the elements of a user story
Understand	• Explain the rationale for focusing on user needs
	• Explain that including too many choices in a user interface increases the cognitive load on users
Apply	• Illustrate the specific users of the system
	• Write descriptions of users that can be used for design
	• Interpret key user needs

THE CONTEXT-OF-USE DESCRIPTION

We need to describe the context of use for several reasons, the two most important being: to support the design of the product, and to support evaluation of the product. The ISO/IEC 25063:2014 standard provides a useful checklist of all the things that might be covered by the context-of-use description. Bearing in mind that only those things have to be documented that will actually be significant for design or evaluation, the list includes:

1. **Scope**[1]
   - What is the system for?
   - What constraints are there on the design of the system?

- Who are the significant distinctly different user groups?
- What other stakeholders could have an impact on the use of the system?
- What are the key constraints of each user group which will affect their relationship with the system?

2. Users

- Demographics such as such as age, gender or education
- Psychological and social characteristics such as cognitive abilities, cultural aspects
- Background, language, literacy, knowledge and skills, motivation and attitude
- Physical and sensory characteristics such as body dimensions, handedness, visual and auditory abilities

3. Goals

- Goals and responsibilities of the user groups and the organisation
- Intended outcomes (including personal goals) that people in each stakeholder group are trying to accomplish
- Any relevant goals of the design organisation (i.e. you, as opposed to your customer)

4. Tasks of each user group

- Description of each task
- For each task: the goal, the result or outcome; whether there is discretion in how to carry out the task; duration, frequency, complexity

5. Technical, social and physical environment(s)

- Elements of the technological environment, for example tools, equipment, hardware configuration, input device(s), network connection, assistive technologies
- Aspects of the social and organisational environment, for example availability of assistance, responsibilities, group dynamics, time pressures, interruptions
- Physical environment – time, location, workplace, lighting, temperature

6. Problems

- Any identified problems that are observed or reported, which could help identify user needs and potential improvements

When aiming for compliance with a standard, there is a temptation to treat it as an exact formal template. This is not the intention – the list is a starting point and a reminder in case things are forgotten. Rather than creating a word-processed document with paragraphs of description under each heading, it is more helpful to produce some of the graphical or semi-graphical artefacts described in the rest of this chapter, which convey the results of user research to development teams in a way that maximises empathy for the end users and focuses the effort.

PERSONAS

One way of pulling together what we currently know, or think we know, about the users of our product is to use **personas**. This technique is attributed to Alan Cooper (2004), although its roots lie further back, in techniques used in marketing. A UX persona has nothing to do with the normal English use of the term; the basic idea is based on the psychology of design and development teams. For team members to achieve an intuitive understanding of the users, the most effective approach is to create an archetype of each group – a symbolic figure whom team members can easily picture in their mind's eye and refer to by their name, rather than talking about abstractly defined user groups.

A persona, then, is a named fictitious person who represents a group. What do we mean by a group, and how do we identify these groups? This brings us back to a point mentioned in Chapter 3: the importance of focusing our design. It is very difficult to design a useful product or service that meets the needs of everyone in the world, because people's needs and attributes vary so much. We can generally only succeed in creating something useful and usable if we focus on a clearly defined population of users – that is, a set of people who all have attributes and needs in common.

Definition: user group

A subset of intended users who are differentiated from other intended users by characteristics of the users, tasks or environments that could influence usability (ISO 9241-11)

The more homogeneous the user population, the more opportunity we have to tailor the product exactly to fit their goals and environments; thus the ideal number of personas we would be designing for would be one. In reality, there are often commercial or organisational reasons why we must consider the needs of more than one group, but the fewer, the better. We can usually distinguish one of them as the most essential: this is the **primary persona**, which takes priority over the others.

More than one primary persona?

If there are two or more user groups that seem to have an equally strong case for being the primary persona, consider whether in fact their needs are different enough to be distinct personas. If so, then you will probably want to create two separate interfaces, one for each group.

It is also sometimes useful to create **negative** personas (also known as *anti-personas*) – outlining for the sake of clarity the types of user that we have decided that the system is *not* going to be designed to support.

Professional UX practice over the years has often involved creating carefully constructed and beautifully documented persona descriptions. These typically include at least:

- Name

- Photograph (usually obtained from a stock photography service)

- Age

- Location

- Employment status

- A soundbite exemplifying the individual's motivations or attitudes

- A description of the individual's goals and behaviours that are relevant to their potential use of the product

- Optionally, various further items, such as socio-economic status or computer literacy level

Traditional customer profiles, as used in marketing, look similar but focus on the demographic details, such as age and socio-economic profile. To use personas effectively, it is vital to appreciate that these are in fact the least important parts of the description. Equally, details such as the name and photograph are of no significance in themselves; they are only there to help the team use the persona. The important points are the descriptions of the user's motivations (their goals), their behaviours, the tools that they are using and the problems that they are encountering – in other words, the items that are specified in ISO/IEC 25063:2014, as described earlier in this chapter.

Because it takes significant effort to develop a set of personas and document them in the format described above, and because companies have often commissioned this work from specialist agencies who naturally charge a significant fee, there is often a desire to re-use persona descriptions across multiple projects. This unfortunately reinforces a tendency that already existed, to treat persona descriptions as a sacrosanct and unchangeable text. The most fruitful approach is exactly the opposite: to keep on questioning and refining the persona descriptions, as your team gradually finds out more about your customers.

The map is not the territory

There can be a tendency to mistake documentation for reality. Just as business analysts sometimes talk about 'requirements' when they actually mean 'requirements documentation', UX people sometimes talk about 'personas' when they really mean 'persona descriptions'. It seems like a trivial distinction, but in fact it is important to remember that the documentation is only a map, not the territory itself. Easy though it may be to forget, our context-of-use descriptions are of little significance in themselves: what matters is our users, and our team's understanding of them.

The reason why developing persona descriptions is expensive is that they need to be based on research. It is sadly very common for organisations to invent a set of personas from thin air and behave as if they were based on something more substantial. These have been referred to, not undeservedly, as 'bullshit personas' as well as '**assumption**

personas' (Sharon, 2016) and can be positively harmful if they point the team in the wrong direction and there is no mechanism for correcting the mistakes. If you are following the approach described in this book, you will not have this problem, because you can build your personas directly from the information you have gathered on field visits.

On the other hand, it is an exaggeration to say that a persona can never be any use if it is not based on research. A more realistic approach is the 'Lean UX' (Gothelf and Seiden, 2013) technique of *proto-personas*. Here, the team creates very rough persona descriptions (Figure 5.1) to guide the work in the first project iterations, on the explicit

Figure 5.1 Persona description

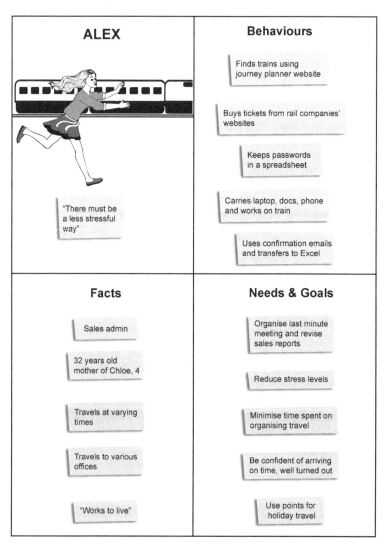

understanding that these are based on assumptions which will probably be falsified. At the first opportunity, the team carries out research that allows the initial set of personas to be thrown away, or radically changed. This is not the end of the process – the personas are continually changed and updated during the project as new information becomes available. The persona description can continue to be documented in a rough form, because this encourages the required experimental attitude. It is the job of user researchers to ensure that the team does continue to deepen and extend its knowledge of the users throughout the course of the work.

JOURNEY MAPS AND STORY MAPS

In Chapter 4, we described how observations written on sticky notes can be grouped together into an affinity diagram, which enables us to see a logical structure emerging from an amorphous mass of data. There is another way of arranging observations that gives a specific and valuable meaning to the data: namely, if we arrange them according to the *time* dimension. This is the underlying principle for a range of techniques with names such as 'maps', 'journeys', 'journey maps' or variations on these terms. It is possible to divide these diagram types into numerous categories (Kalbach, 2016) but what they have in common is more important than what distinguishes them. We refer to these diagrams as *journey maps* (Figure 5.2).

Figure 5.2 Journey map

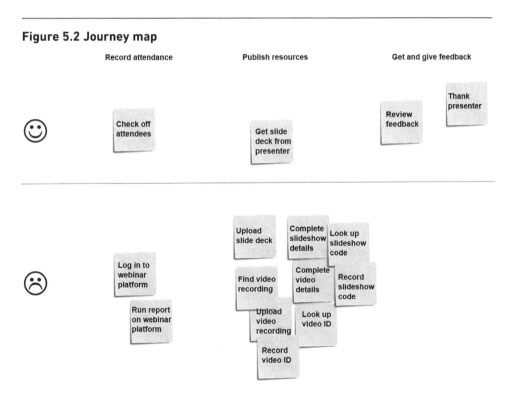

Journey maps are usually arranged along an axis that runs from left to right, representing time. The map consists of a number of episodes that collectively tell a story about either:

- the experience that one research participant has described to us or that we have observed;
- an aggregation of several individuals' experiences in relation to the same thing; or
- the general experience that we would like users of our product or service to have in the future.

A journey map can describe a short experience, such as making a purchase on a website, or a longer experience that might last months, years or even decades, such as being the owner of a specific model of car or the customer of a particular hotel chain.

Because only one of the two available diagramming dimensions is used to represent time, the other is available for representing further information. Sometimes it is used to represent the user's affective state, where the top of the chart represents positive feelings and the bottom represents negative ones. Sometimes the diagram is divided into horizontal bands, each being used to represent a different type of information regarding each episode, for example:

- As on an empathy map, what the user sees, hears and feels.
- As in AEIOU, what environment the user is in, what people or organisational units they interact with, and what equipment or software user interface components they use.
- The different levels of visible and invisible organisational and technological support for episodes in the user journey – this is referred to as a service blueprint.

Journey maps are an immensely useful tool for visualising, comparing and analysing experiences. They sometimes bear a superficial resemblance to activity diagrams or business process models, but there is a profound difference: journey maps aim to understand the experience from the human users' subjective point of view, whereas activity diagrams and business process models aim to show an objective overall representation based on the notion of a piece of work flowing through the system.

User journey maps and user story maps

A user story map (Figure 5.3) is similar to a user journey map, but it is created for a very specific reason – to organise development activity rather than to describe the users' current experience. See the description of **user stories** later in this chapter for more details.

Figure 5.3 Story map

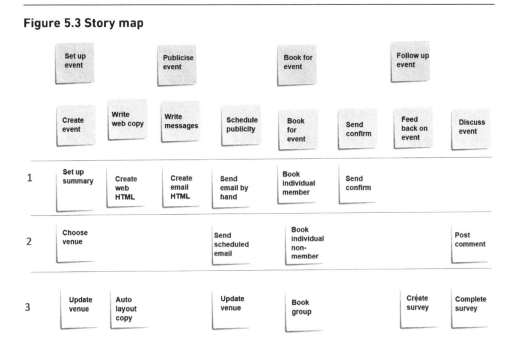

SCENARIOS

A scenario is a story describing a typical situation that might be experienced by a member of one of our user groups. In the same way that personas help the project team to understand and relate intuitively to the users, scenarios help the team to maintain a proper understanding of required solution functionality, by telling a story that is complete with realistic details of the environment. Scenarios are a perfect fit with persona descriptions – together, they paint a compelling picture of the problems that people encounter in trying to achieve their goals, and how a given design might improve things.

Scenarios can be documented in a range of ways. Like so many of the other techniques in this book, they are most useful when kept short and simple. A brief textual description is very easy to produce. An even more vivid illustration can sometimes be provided by drawing a cartoon-like storyboard or comic strip. Even for those of us with few artistic skills, it is surprisingly easy to do this using a few simple ideas (Cheng, 2012; Greenberg et al., 2011).

USER NEEDS

Personas and scenarios help us to understand the context of use correctly by providing realistic detail in a structured way. User needs, on the other hand, allow us to focus clearly on the users' tasks and goals by articulating them in a very concise way.

'User needs' can be a technical term

Quite often, the term 'user needs' is used in a very general way to refer to the functionality that users need, and is a synonym for 'user requirements'. As Kim Goodwin (2011) points out, this choice of language is sometimes a subtle way for UX people to gain a greater measure of influence over requirements definition by using their own terminology.

However, in this book we use it in a more restricted and specific sense, as described below. This is the interpretation of 'user needs' used by the UK Government (GOV. UK, 2017).

A user need describes something that a user needs (or wants) to do. It is a high-level objective, independent of any details of how the objective might be achieved using any particular solution.

A user need is expressed in 'user story format':

As a [user role]
I need/want to [do this task]
so that [I can achieve this goal]

The simplicity and rigour of this format is valuable, as it forces us to think clearly about who the user is and what goals they are seeking to achieve. The best user need descriptions are expressed using wording that would realistically be used by the users themselves, not using tech-speak. A user need description should be about the user and what they want to achieve, not about the system.

KEY TASKS

Users can have many needs. On most projects, numerous ideas will come up about functionality that should be provided. Each set of stakeholders will have their own ideas and priorities: business owners, product managers and developers all want to give their input. User research is likely to throw up quite a range of possibilities. However, one of the worst mistakes we can make when designing a system is to try to please everyone – by taking this approach, we are likely to end up pleasing no one. Even if we focus our design on a single persona, there may be a very large set of functionality envisaged.

Hick's law is one of the few well-known scientific findings that have a clear and undisputed significance for user experience design. If we think about a simple list of links displayed on a web page navigation control, it is easy to see that the more links there are to choose from, the harder it will be to find the right one. But the principle is far more widely applicable than that. The fact is that the fewer functions a system provides, the easier it is to use. The marginal effect of every new added feature may be insignificant on its own, but eventually the cumulative effect of too much functionality is to make a system unusable.

We need an effective way of paring down the mass of proposed functionality to the essentials. One useful idea comes from user experience consultant David Travis (2006) with the concept of *Red Routes*. This is based on the analogy of London's road system, where certain roads have been identified as the key arteries that keep circulation going in the city's traffic system. Red lines are painted on these roads and the authorities are zealous in ensuring that no obstacles to traffic, such as parked cars, are allowed even for a minute. Similarly, we can identify red routes in a website. These are complete journeys through the website that allow users to achieve the goals that they set out to do when they came to the site. They are defined in terms of outcomes that users value. They are likely to be activities that are critically important to users or to the business (or both) and may well be activities that are carried out frequently. Identify these, and we will know the journeys that the system simply must support as well as possible. All other design considerations must be subordinated to this, probably to the extent of leaving out (or making less visible) nice-to-have functionality that makes the red routes harder to navigate.

Hick's law

The time taken to make a decision increases as the number of choices is expanded.

USER STORIES

A user story represents a unit of development work that needs to be done. It is a tool for managing the backlog of work that remains to be done at any given time on an Agile project. User stories are not 'stories' in the usual sense of the word, but they are orientated towards users: each user story describes something that has value for a given user group because it helps them to achieve their goals.

We have already seen the user story format, when discussing user needs. A user need is a high-level user story.

User stories are the crucial link between user experience design and software design. If they are framed in the right way, making full use of the personas, goals, tasks and scenarios discovered in user research, they make a massive contribution towards delivering a useful and usable product.

User story maps are a technique for helping a development team to decide how to order the work in such a way as to deliver value in each project iteration. Because a key consideration is the need to create a coherent set of functions that support users in achieving their goals, it follows that the stories are arranged into a time-ordered sequence, and so the resulting map looks very much like any other user journey map.

User story format

User stories are not really documents: they consist of all the thinking, conversations and decision-making that has taken place within the development team relating to the unit of work in question. However, they are traditionally summarised on *user story cards*. Strictly speaking, there are no hard and fast rules about the format of user story cards, but the format described in this section has become so common that it is sometimes called 'user story format'. This is known to developers as the role–feature–reason template. From a UX perspective, we might prefer to call it the user–task–goal format:

- **As a** [user role]
- **I need/want to** [do this task]
- **So that** [I can achieve this goal]

SUMMARY

The context of use consists of the users, their tasks and goals, their resources and their environment.

The users of a system and, to some extent, all the other context-of-use items can be illustrated by defining personas – fictitious archetypes that represent the key user groups, concentrating on their behaviours and needs. The development of the users' experience over time within their environment can be documented in user journey maps and scenarios.

Having achieved a rich and detailed view of the context of use, we need to narrow our focus to the most important things. Defining user needs is the first step towards this.

As Hick's law states, 'The time taken to make a decision increases as the number of choices is expanded.' The simpler a system's user interface, the more usable it has the potential to be. It should be optimised for the users' key tasks – those that are frequent and result in valuable outcomes.

User stories encapsulate desired functionality and are written in the form, 'As a [user role], I need/want to [do this task], so that [I can achieve this goal]'. Defining user stories allows us to start moving towards creating design solutions based on a solid understanding of the context of use.

NOTE

1. 'Scope' is not strictly an element of the context of use, as defined by ISO 9241-11. The items under this section relate to the goals (first bullet point), environment (second point) and users (remaining points) respectively.

REFERENCES

Cheng, K. (2012) *See What I Mean: How to Use Comics to Communicate Ideas.* Rosenfeld Media, New York.

Cooper, A. (2004) *The Inmates are Running the Asylum: Why High-Tech Products Drive Us Crazy and How to Restore the Sanity*. SAMS, Indianapolis, IN.

de Saint-Exupéry, A. (1939) *Terre des hommes*. Gallimard, Lagny-sur-Marne.

Gothelf, J. and Seiden, J. (2013) *Lean UX: Applying Lean Principles to Improve User Experience*. O'Reilly Media, Sebastopol, CA.

Goodwin, K. (2011) *Designing for the Digital Age: How to Create Human-Centered Products and Services*. Wiley, Indianapolis, IN.

GOV.UK (2017) *Learning About Users and Their Needs*. Available from: https://www.gov.uk/service-manual/user-research/start-by-learning-user-needs

Greenberg, S., Carpendale, S., Marquardt, N. and Buxton, B. (2011) *Sketching User Experiences: The Workbook*. Elsevier, Waltham, MA.

ISO/IEC 25063:2014 (2014) *Systems and Software Engineering – Systems and Software Quality Requirements and Evaluation (SQuaRE) – Common Industry Format (CIF) for Usability: Context of Use Description*. International Organization for Standardization (ISO), Geneva.

Kalbach, J. (2016) *Mapping Experiences: A Complete Guide to Creating Value Through Journeys, Blueprints, and Diagrams*. O'Reilly Media, Sebastopol, CA.

Sharon, T. (2016) *Validating Product Ideas: Through Lean User Research*. Rosenfeld Media, New York.

Travis, D. (2006) *Red Route Usability: The Key User Journeys with your Web Site*. Available from: https://www.userfocus.co.uk/articles/redroutes.html

FURTHER READING

Cooper, A., Reimann, R., Cronin, D. and Noessel, C. (2014) *About Face: The Essentials of Interaction Design*. Wiley, Indianapolis, IN.

Patton, J. and Economy, P. (2014) *User Story Mapping: Discover the Whole Story, Build the Right Product*. O'Reilly Media, Sebastopol, CA.

Pruitt, J. and Adlin, T. (2006) *The Persona Lifecycle: Keeping People in Mind throughout Product Design*. Morgan Kaufmann, San Francisco, CA.

Travis, D. (2002) *E-Commerce Usability: Tools and Techniques to Perfect the On-Line Experience*. Taylor & Francis, London.

EXAMPLE EXAMINATION QUESTIONS

1. **You are working on a government system that allows people to apply for a driving licence. Which of the following would be examples of user needs for such a service?**

   a. It should be easy to navigate

   b. The font size should be at least 12 pt

   c. Apply for provisional entitlement to drive a lorry

   d. It should work on mobile devices as well as desktop computers

2. **You are designing an interface for a government system that will be used by a large number of users. Which design approach would be MOST LIKELY to be successful?**

   a. Administer a survey to at least 1000 potential users to uncover the key demographic characteristics

   b. Include a wide range of functions to suit most people

   c. Emulate design patterns from high traffic, social networking sites

   d. Design for specific groups of users with specific needs

3. **A new application is proposed that enables individuals to look up all bus services within a small city. Which of the following would be the BEST user description to be used in the system design?**

   a. A commuter who uses three buses a day each way to get to work, with short intervals to change between buses

   b. A 27-year-old bus spotter, who is interested in the cumulative late running of services

   c. Police traffic control staff, interested in the effect of roadworks and traffic lights on services

   d. An inspector for a bus operating company who wants to check on the performance of individual drivers

4. **Identify the key user needs in this pen portrait of a user for a GPS system aimed at hikers:**

   1. Peter has been a keen walker since he was a teenager.

   2. He enjoys purchasing the latest gadgets and technology.

   3. He wants to discover out-of-the-way sites with an interesting history.

   4. He says he needs a mobile phone provider with better coverage in out-of-the-way locations.

      a. 1 and 2 only

      b. 2 only

      c. 3 and 4 only

      d. 3 only

ANSWERS TO EXAMPLE QUESTIONS

1. The correct answer is (c).

(b) and (d) are non-functional specifications referring to a specific implementation and are not expressions of a user's need from the service. (a) is an abstract requirement that assumes the system will have some kind of navigation. It may not. This leaves (c) as the correct answer.

2. The correct answer is (d).

This question tests candidates' understanding of focusing on users in design. (a) is wrong because demographic characteristics are of only rudimentary use when doing design. (b) is wrong because it will lead to a system that suffers from bloat but still does not meet the needs of users. (c) is wrong because design is contextual, and an approach that works on one site may not work on another. This leaves (d) as the best answer.

3. The correct answer is (a).

This question is about identifying the main user group in the design of a system. All of these groups are potential users of the system, but the question asks the candidate to identify the best user description; that is, the group that is most likely to have a need for the service. Option (a) is more realistic (in terms of genuine use), so this gives the best answer. This is not to invalidate the use of a bus spotter as a potential user – but people in this category are not using the service as the majority of people would – 'is my bus on time and likely to get me to my destination as required?' Option (c) is another likely secondary user group, but again will not be the main user of the service (that is, the service should not be designed specifically for this audience). Option (d) is another possible secondary user, although this user will almost certainly require other data (such as driver names) alongside the timetable.

4. The correct answer is (d).

A good user need will begin with a word like 'needs' or 'wants'. Although (1) is useful information for a persona, it is not a user need: it simply captures a little of the user's domain knowledge. Similarly, (2) is not a need but a personality trait. (4) is a possible option, but notice the phrase, 'he says' in the stem. This isn't a need but an implementation. The user need behind this could be met by other implementations (for example, a system that allowed the user to download maps before setting off on the walk). This leaves option (3) as the only user need in the list and makes (d) the correct choice.

6 MEASURING USABILITY

> Civilization advances by extending the number of important operations which we can perform without thinking about them.
>
> Alfred North Whitehead (1911)

INTRODUCTION

This chapter describes how to build a design around objectively measurable concepts so that it can be progressively evaluated and improved using an iterative process. We examine the definition of **usability** and its subsidiary components of **effectiveness**, **accuracy**, **completeness**, **efficiency** and **satisfaction**. We see how these, together with the definition of the context of use, can form the basis for a series of experiments that will guide development. We introduce the Build–Measure–Learn loop and the idea of **validated learning**. To conclude, we show how *split testing*, **A/B testing** and **multivariate testing** can help to generate evidence-based decisions – when used in the right context.

LEARNING OBJECTIVES

After reading this chapter you will be able to:

Remember	• Define usability
	• Recall that users react emotionally to good and bad user experiences
Understand	• Identify the strengths and weaknesses of multivariate testing as a method for choosing between design alternatives
	• Explain the value of iterative design
Apply	• Illustrate how the definition of usability can be used to construct measures of usability
	• Demonstrate how to choose between good and poor design ideas by using behavioural data
	• Illustrate the role design experiments play in validated learning

WHAT IS USABILITY?

When specifying requirements for a system, it is still quite common for people to write things like, 'the system shall have a user-friendly [or intuitive] interface', or 'all information shall be accessible within two mouse clicks'. These are not useful statements of requirements. The first example is impossibly vague and could mean anything. The second at least attempts to be specific, but unfortunately is based on inappropriate preconceptions about what makes a system usable.

We can only be sure of designing a usable system if we have a way of measuring usability precisely. To use a scientific term, we need to *operationalise* the concept of usability. Operationalising a concept means taking something that seems intangible and impossible to measure, and specifying how to measure it. This often involves defining subsidiary elements that split the concept up into parts. The overall effect is to bring the concept into sharper focus.

Besides defining the context of use, the other great contribution of ISO 9241-11 is that it does exactly what we need here: it operationalises the concept of usability by identifying its components and subcomponents to the extent that they can be tested. Hence there is no need for us to flounder around with useless requirements like those quoted above.

Definition: usability

The extent to which a system, product or service can be used by specified **users** to achieve specified **goals** with **effectiveness**, **efficiency** and **satisfaction** in a specified **context of use** (ISO 9241-11, 2018)

The definition contains three items that we have already talked about at some length:

- Users
- Goals
- Context of use (which of course actually includes users and goals)

It introduces three further concepts:

- Effectiveness
- Efficiency
- Satisfaction

Fortunately, these are also carefully defined.

Effectiveness

Definition: effectiveness

The **accuracy** and **completeness** with which users achieve specified goals (ISO 9241-11, 2018)

Accuracy and completeness are most appropriately considered from the user's point of view, rather than the system. We should not be asking whether the system gave accurate or complete output, or whether the user interacted with the system in the correct way, but rather whether the user was able to achieve exactly what they intended, with the help of the system. Accuracy and completeness also each have a definition.

Definition: accuracy

The extent to which an actual outcome matches an intended outcome (ISO 9241-11, 2018)

Definition: completeness

The extent to which users are able to achieve all intended outcomes (ISO 9241-11, 2018)

When the user succeeds in achieving the outcome they intended, it is quite hard to tell the difference between accuracy and completeness. It is easier to see when something goes wrong. For example, if I book two railway tickets for next Tuesday and then find on checking the confirmation email that one of them is for the wrong destination, that is a problem of accuracy. If one of them is missing altogether, that is a failure of completeness.

We can evaluate whether users can achieve their goals accurately and completely by creating a scenario that requires them to achieve a typical goal, asking several typical users to enact the scenario, and then taking measurements, such as:

1. What percentage of users achieved the goal completely?
2. What percentage of users achieved the goal accurately?
3. What percentage of users achieved the goal both completely and accurately? This is sometimes referred to as 'success rate'.
4. If any users did not achieve the goal completely, to what extent did they complete it?
5. If any users did not achieve the goal accurately, how serious were the inaccuracies?

Effectiveness measures are most often reported as percentages.

Efficiency

Definition: efficiency

The resources used in relation to the results achieved (ISO 9241-11, 2018)

As the old saying goes, 'Good, cheap, fast – pick two!' In other words, effectiveness may come at a cost in terms of either money, time or some other scarce resource.

When assessing usability, the resource most often considered is time. As an even older saying goes, 'time is money'. We can evaluate the time taken by users to complete tasks easily enough. Hence, efficiency is most often reported as a length of time measured in seconds.

Other resources that might be considered relevant are cognitive load, goodwill and patience. We can measure cognitive load by testing the participant's ability to carry out some other basic task simultaneously with the task being assessed. Goodwill and patience are usually covered by measuring satisfaction.

Satisfaction

Definition: satisfaction

The extent to which the user's physical, cognitive and emotional responses that result from the use of a system, product or service meet the user's needs and expectations. This includes the extent to which the user experience that results from actual use meets the user's needs and expectations. Anticipated use can influence satisfaction with actual use (ISO 9241-11, 2018)

The definition of satisfaction acknowledges the close link between satisfaction and user experience. Remember that user experience itself is defined as 'a user's perceptions and responses resulting from the use and/or anticipated use of a system, product or service'. What we are testing here, then, is the quality of the user experience resulting from actual use of the product. This includes emotional reactions.

Satisfaction can be measured using the **System Usability Scale** (SUS) (Brooke, 1996). This is a very well-established questionnaire that asks to what extent the user agrees with the following propositions:

1. I think that I would like to use this system frequently.

2. I found the system unnecessarily complex.

3. I thought the system was easy to use.

4. I think that I would need the support of a technical person to be able to use this system.

5. I found the various functions in this system were well integrated.

6. I thought there was too much inconsistency in this system.

7. I would imagine that most people would learn to use this system very quickly.

8. I found the system very cumbersome to use.

9. I felt very confident using the system.

10. I needed to learn a lot of things before I could get going with this system.

A five-point scale from 'Strongly disagree' to 'Strongly agree' is used for responses, which are then converted into a numeric **SUS score**.

Method for measuring usability

We can now see that the ISO 9241-11 definitions give much-needed clarity on how to evaluate and design for usability. We need to:

1. Define the context of use, as described in the previous two chapters.

2. Create an evaluation environment that enables us to mirror the context of use.

3. Define acceptable levels of accuracy, completeness, efficiency and satisfaction.

4. Have users, or people who are qualified to represent users in accordance with step 1, attempt to carry out tasks to achieve their goals in that environment, using the designs we have created.

5. Assess whether the target levels were achieved.

Other dimensions of usability

Some other aspects of a system's usability are identified by ISO 9241-11. These include two measures related to commonly encountered goals of direct and indirect users respectively:

- Learnability: how well does the system support the goal of learning to use it? Arguably this includes memorability – how well does the system support the goal of remembering how to use it between episodes of use?

- Maintainability: how well does the system support the goals of maintaining it?

The standard also identifies some other outcomes of system use that are not considered part of usability, but are highly relevant:

- Accessibility: how usable is the system by people with a wide range of needs? This is discussed further in Chapter 11.

- Avoidance of harm from use: what negative consequences might arise from using the system?

These are shown as further measures in Figure 6.1.

Figure 6.1 Measures of usability

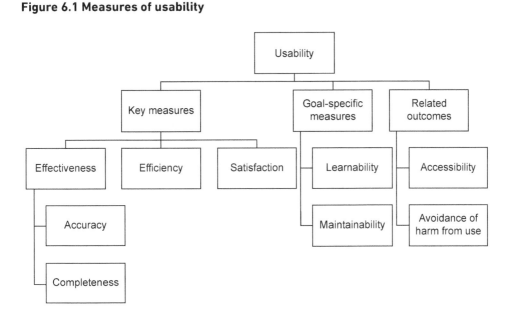

ITERATIVE DESIGN IN A USER-CENTRED PROCESS

The method for testing usability described above will allow us to evaluate one particular design. However, being able to evaluate one design falls a long way short of guaranteeing a good final product. Many products and systems are inherently complex. A system's fitness for purpose is the result of even more complex interactions among its intrinsic properties, the users' characteristics, behaviours and motivations, their goals, and all the other elements of the social, physical and technical environment. We can only hope to achieve a good end product by proceeding with comparatively small steps and testing as we go. This is why user-centred design is iterative, as described in Chapter 3.

Validated learning

In *The Lean Startup* (2011), Eric Ries describes an approach to dealing with uncertainty in business based on the experimental method. Recognising the importance of assumptions in any enterprise that is based on creating something new, Ries proposes using **validated learning** as the driving principle in developing innovative solutions.

In a nutshell, validated learning means identifying assumptions that you are making, and immediately designing experiments to find out whether they are justified or not, making the 'feedback loop' as short as possible. Ries structures his approach as a cycle with three phases: Build–Measure–Learn. This fits perfectly with the iterative nature of user-centred design. The shorter the feedback loop, the more learning cycles we are able to go through, and ultimately the more we can learn, providing we make a systematic effort to prioritise learning.

To test an assumption, we need to reframe it as a hypothesis: in a defined set of circumstances, if a certain thing happens, then a certain thing will be the result. We can identify two key types of hypothesis that are relevant. The first is the *problem hypothesis*. This represents our idea that certain users have a particular problem when it comes to achieving their goals in certain environments. We can carry out user research to find out whether this is true or not. This is targeted research designed as an experiment, to give maximum clarity and certainty about whether the assumption is correct. The details of the experiment will depend very much on the type of the problem, but will involve gathering quantitative data on user behaviour, rather than opinions or preferences. We may well iterate through several different design hypotheses before settling on one. Proto-personas, as described in Chapter 5, are part of this.

A *solution hypothesis* is defined in terms of how a particular design concept might help the users to achieve their goals, by simplifying their tasks or reframing the problem. This can also be tested by user research, preferably based on carrying out usability testing (see Chapter 11) using a prototype (see Chapter 10). Again, we will hope to cycle through many solution hypotheses during a project.

A design hypothesis is a proposition that can be supported or proven to be false by a *design experiment*. In principle (real experiments will often be less formal than this) it will be structured like this:

- if we provide tool <T> with functionality <f>
- user <u> will be able to achieve goal <g> in environment <e>
- in time <t> or with satisfaction <s> and so on

The key questions to ask at the beginning of each cycle are:

- Identifying the next hypothesis: 'What is the most important thing we need to learn at this stage? Which assumption is the riskiest? Which assumption will cause the entire idea to fail if it is mistaken?'
- Designing the experiment: 'What is the smallest amount of work we can possibly do to learn the most important thing? How can we get an answer as fast as possible?'

Split testing

Another way of testing design ideas is to carry out multivariate testing or A/B testing. These are two flavours of a general technique known as split testing. In split testing, two or more different designs are given to different visitors as part of their experience with a live website. Special-purpose software is able to direct a given proportion of web server requests to each variation on the design – this may be as simple as two versions of the same web page with one very localised difference, or it may be a sequence of entirely different pages. 'A/B testing' is sometimes used to describe an experiment where versions of an entire web page are contrasted with each other, whereas 'multivariate testing' can specifically refer to more fine-grained testing where many permutations of variants on detailed elements are compared. Some visitors see one version, and some see another, without even knowing about it, and the results are then analysed to see which was more successful in helping the users to achieve their goals.

Split testing is an example of a purely evidence-based, data-driven design approach. In principle, techniques like this allow us to make good design decisions without wasting time in pointless arguments on the basis of unsubstantiated opinions. Once the necessary technical environment is set up for running split-testing experiments, it is possible to run very many experiments at scale.

Split testing is only useful in the context of a live web-based service that has a very large number of users. If only a few users are involved, the results will lack statistical significance. Another feature of split testing is that it gives no insight into the reason why one design is more effective than another, only the extent to which the outcome varies. It is useful when fine-tuning the details of the design in the later stages of a project. As a technique that generates decisions rather than new possibilities, it is an example of convergent as opposed to divergent thinking (see Chapter 12).

SUMMARY

Usability is defined as 'the extent to which a system, product or service can be used by specified users to achieve specified goals with effectiveness, efficiency and satisfaction in a specified context of use' (ISO 9241-11, 2018). Usability can be measured objectively by measuring the components of this definition in a controlled way.

A user's experience with a system will inevitably generate an emotional reaction. Satisfaction, which measures this, is the most subjective component of usability. However, it can be evaluated using a standard survey.

The team's progression towards the delivery of a valuable end product needs to be conceived of as a learning journey. With each cycle of the user-centred process, they must undertake validated learning: identify the most important areas of uncertainty, then create hypotheses and design experiments to gain the understanding they need.

Split testing, including A/B testing and multivariate testing, automates the assessment of alternative designs' relative strengths, and allows decisions to be taken on the basis of facts rather than opinions, but it does not give any insight into the reasons why one design performs better than another.

REFERENCES

Brooke, J. (1996) SUS: a quick and dirty usability scale. In Jordan, P.W., Thomas, B., Weerdmeester, B.A. and McClelland, I.L. (eds), *Usability Evaluation in Industry*. Taylor & Francis, London.

ISO 9241-11:2018 (2018) *Ergonomics of Human-System Interaction – Part 11: Usability: Definitions and Concepts*. International Organization for Standardization (ISO), Geneva.

Ries, E. (2011) *The Lean Startup: How Today's Entrepreneurs Use Continuous Innovation to Create Radically Successful Businesses*. Penguin, London.

Whitehead, A.N. (1911) *An Introduction to Mathematics*. Cambridge University Press, Cambridge.

FURTHER READING

Albert, W. and Tullis, T. (2013) *Measuring the User Experience: Collecting, Analyzing, and Presenting Usability Metrics.* Newnes, Oxford.

Gothelf, J. and Seiden, J. (2013) *Lean UX: Applying Lean Principles to Improve User Experience.* O'Reilly Media, Sebastopol, CA.

Travis, D. (2002) *E-Commerce Usability: Tools and Techniques to Perfect the On-Line Experience.* Taylor & Francis, London.

EXAMPLE EXAMINATION QUESTIONS

1. **Which of the following aspects of usability are MOST important for each scenario? Match the choices.**

    1. An online multiplayer game used by teenagers
    2. A fingerprint identification system used by trained police officers
    3. A kiosk in a museum that helps visitors find an exhibit
    4. A call logging system used by trained call centre operatives
    W. Task completion rate
    X. Time to complete the task
    Y. A rating scale to measure satisfaction with the task
    Z. A count of the number of incorrect decisions
        a. 1Y, 2Z, 3W, 4X
        b. 1Z, 2Y, 3X, 4W
        c. 1X, 2W, 3Y, 4Z
        d. 1Y, 2X, 3Z, 4W

2. **What role do design experiments play when creating products?**

    a. Design experiments help the design team validate their learning about customers
    b. Design experiments encourage the design team to get face to face with users
    c. Design experiments guarantee that design decisions are statistically significant
    d. Design experiments ensure that the development team is working within an Agile framework

ANSWERS TO EXAMPLE QUESTIONS

1. The correct answer is (a).

It's true that task completion rate is an important measure for all systems, but (2) and (4) are systems used by expert users and these people will have the experience or training to complete the tasks. Efficiency is most important in a call centre task, which is why (X) is the best choice. With games, part of the enjoyment is becoming immersed in the task, so task completion, time to complete and incorrect decisions are poor metrics: satisfaction (Y) is the best choice. For the fingerprint system, all of these measures are important but (Z) is the best choice because incorrect decisions could lead to identifying the wrong suspect. Option (a) is therefore the preferred answer.

2. The correct answer is (a).

Option (d) is not correct since teams can practise Agile without carrying out design experiments (and vice versa). Option (c) is incorrect because the results from design experiments do not need to be statistically significant to be useful (often teams are just looking to see which way the wind blows). Although (b) is partly true, a team can carry out a design experiment without directly engaging with a user (e.g. A/B testing). This leaves (a) as the correct answer.

7 INFORMATION ARCHITECTURE

> The most important component to design properly is ... the user's conceptual model. Everything else should be subordinated to making that model clear, obvious and substantial. That is almost exactly the opposite of how most software is designed.
>
> David Liddle, lead designer of the Xerox Star system (1996)

INTRODUCTION

This chapter defines the discipline of **information architecture** and discusses some of its key concepts. We examine five different ways in which information can be organised and present the LATCH mnemonic for remembering them. We describe how to do **card sorting**, an objective method for ensuring that we organise the content and functions of a user interface in a way that makes sense to users. We discuss three different types of models of a system – the **mental model**, **conceptual model** and **implementation model** – and define the concept of **affordance**.

LEARNING OBJECTIVES

After reading this chapter you will be able to:

Remember	• State the concept of affordance
Understand	• Recognise the way information flows between a person and a product or service
	• Describe the steps in carrying out an open and closed card sort
	• Compare and contrast an implementation model, a mental model and a conceptual model
Apply	• Choose appropriate schemes for classifying and organising information
	• Organise, structure and label content, functions and features

WHAT IS INFORMATION ARCHITECTURE?

Chapters 8 and 9 discuss aspects of detailed design – the nuts and bolts of what makes a user interface usable or otherwise. But there is no point paying attention to the details if we do not also think about the big picture – how the user thinks about the product or service as a whole, and how they find information and functionality. These are the concerns of the **information architecture** (IA) discipline: ensuring that **users** can understand the interface and find the functions, features or content they need to achieve their **tasks.**

A user's interaction with a product, system or service is a conversation that progresses through a series of stages. We can think of the conversation as a two-way flow of information. At each stage, the user has to make sense of what the system is about, what resources and options are being offered, and what action and information is expected from them in order to reach the next stage. We must design the system so that the user always has sufficient information to understand the current state of the conversation and to proceed to the next stage.

For this to happen,

- The resources available via the interface must be organised in a way that is adapted to the kinds of task that the users will be carrying out. The next section, 'Organisational schemes for Information', describes a way of making sure that we take a broad view when thinking about this.

- Not only should the organisational scheme be objectively suitable for carrying out the tasks, it should also match the way that the users think about them. The 'Card sorting' section presents a technique that helps with this.

- The way that the system appears to work should match the way that users expect it to work, and both should match the way it actually does work. We use the terms conceptual model, mental model and implementation model to denote these three things, as described under 'Mental, conceptual and implementation models', below.

At a more detailed level, the elements of the user interface must be presented in a way that makes their purpose evident, as described under 'Affordances', below.

ORGANISATIONAL SCHEMES FOR INFORMATION

How exactly do you come to be reading this particular page of this book? Maybe you are reading it from cover to cover, and this is the point you have reached in that sequential journey. Perhaps there was a bookmark or sticky note indicating this page, allowing you to go directly to it. Perhaps you looked up a term such as 'information architecture' in the Index. Or maybe you browsed through the list of headings in the Contents and decided to dip in here. These all represent time-honoured alternative ways of accessing the same information in a printed book. Equally, when we design a service or information system of any sort, we need to provide a carefully chosen set of ways for people to understand what they are dealing with, to grasp its scope and structure, and to find information and functionality in various circumstances.

Richard Saul Wurman (2000) proposes a taxonomy of organisational schemes for information and offers the acronym 'LATCH' for remembering them.

- **Location**: A list of headings indicating towns, countries or other geographical areas organises information according to location. A map not only does that, but it makes it possible to see and explore geographical or spatial relationships. When the user is looking for a resource relating to a given location, a map is the natural way of showing an overview of possibilities. If the device is location-aware, it can automatically show a map of the resources closest to the user's current location. A display based on a smaller scale can help the user to explore a complicated structure, such as a machine or biological organism.

- **Alphabet**: Alphabetical order is a good default scheme when no other scheme seems to suggest itself, especially when there is a large amount of data to sort.

- **Time**: Time, or date, is often a natural way of ordering a list of information items that represent past or future events. For example, a list of email messages could be ordered by 'Time Sent'. Using time as an organisational scheme and mapping it onto a spatial representation makes it possible to display and compare information about sequence, duration and frequency in a graphical form.

- **Category**: For any given set of items that needs to be organised and presented, there is likely to be a choice of various attributes, types or categories that could be used. For example, the same list of email messages could be filtered or searched by 'Subject' or 'Sender'.

- **Hierarchy**: It might have been more appropriate to name this item 'Rank', but that would not make a good acronym. Wurman does not mean a 'hierarchical' arrangement like the structure of a chart showing reporting lines within a company. He is instead referring to any organisational scheme based on comparative ranking, such as 'Price', 'Size' or 'Rating'. Hierarchy in the more common sense is also used as an organisational scheme – for example, as described in the discussion on card sorting below.

CARD SORTING

A very popular organisational scheme used for both the pages of websites and the functionality of software applications is a hierarchical arrangement, where the individual pages or commands are organised into named groups. In its simplest form, this leads to a two-level navigation structure consisting of the group names on the first level, with the items themselves on the second level. When there is a lot of content, the groups themselves are organised into higher-level groups, resulting in a hierarchy with three or more levels. However, it is generally the case that the more levels there are, the more likely users are to become disorientated and fail to achieve their intended goal.

How can we decide what names to give the groups in such a way as to maximise the chances of the user finding what they are looking for? The answer is to use **card sorting**, another wonderful user research technique for making decisions on the basis of objective evidence about users, rather than the designer's opinion. There are two types of card sort:

- An **open card sort**, where participants decide on the groups for themselves.

- A **closed card sort**, where participants assign each item to one of a predefined set of groups.

The two techniques can be used in conjunction with each other, with an open sort followed by a closed sort. The steps in this method are as follows, as summarised in Figure 7.1.

Figure 7.1 Key steps in conducting a card sorting exercise

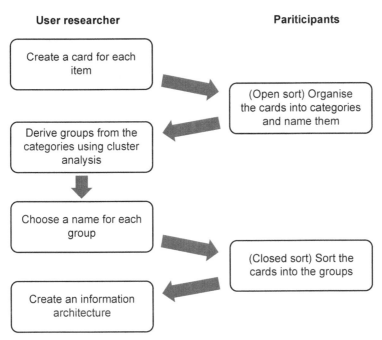

1. **The user researcher creates a card for each item:** Create a set of cards (or pieces of paper), one set per participant. These should be roughly the size of index cards or A6. Print on each card the name or description of the item. This should be expressed in clear, neutral language as concisely as possible. You should be prepared to explain the meaning of the item names to participants if they ask. If this happens, make a note of it.

2. **(Open sort) The participants organise the cards into categories and name them:** Ask the users to put the cards into as many groups as they think appropriate. Once they have finished, ask them to use a blank card to write a name for each group that they have created. The name does not necessarily have to be concise: it just has to clarify what this group of items have in common. Record all the information on the groups in a spreadsheet or special-purpose software tool.

3. **The user researcher derives groups from the categories using cluster analysis:** The next stage is to come up with a set of groups that represents the consensus view on the most appropriate set of groups. There is a mathematical technique for this called **monothetic agglomerative cluster analysis**, which identifies which cards are most often assigned to the same group as each other. In most cases, there will be a reasonably clear consensus. If two or more different schemes emerge as equally strong contenders, there may be a case for providing alternative navigation schemes.

4. **The user researcher chooses a name for each group**: For each item, we need to identify the most effective *trigger word* that will be noticed and automatically associated with the relevant subject matter by the maximum number of people. Ideally, the group names written by the open card sort participants will do most of this work.

5. **(Closed sort) The participants sort the cards into the groups**: We now need to test the set of groups that the cluster analysis has given us, to ensure that it does actually work. This can be done by running a closed sort with a different set of participants, where we use the same card deck but ask the participants to place the cards into the groups that we have defined. If there are any discrepancies at this point, it will be necessary to revisit some of the previous steps.

6. **The user researcher creates an information architecture**: the final step is to create the real information architecture on the basis of the research.

When doing 'real world' face-to-face card sorting, it is most efficient to have several participants in the room simultaneously, as this cuts down on the time needed for briefing and debriefing them. Each individual should carry out the task without communicating with the others, however, as that would compromise the authenticity of the results. Card sorting can also be done online, which allows all the data collection and analysis to be done automatically.

MENTAL, CONCEPTUAL AND IMPLEMENTATION MODELS

Card sorting is effective because it enables the researcher to see, in a simple way, the thought processes of users. This information is immensely valuable. One of the biggest obstacles to designing usable systems is the difficulty that designers have in understanding the user's **mental model**.

Although cognitive scientists disagree about the details, it is generally agreed that people have a representation in their mind of any system that they interact with. This is a kind of model that they use to understand and predict the behaviour of the system. If the user's mental model is accurate, they will be good at using the system. If not, then the result will be ineffective use and frustration.

By contrast, the **conceptual model** is the model that the designers create when defining and refining the solution hypothesis. This is a small but coherent set of ideas about 'how the system works', reflecting the designers' conclusions on the best way of emphasising some concepts and hiding others, and also reflecting the nature of the users' perception of their tasks in the structure of what they see, hear and feel when using the product. This is a two-way process: the system design needs to reflect the user's perception of the task domain, with the objects and actions that it contains; but equally, the model presented to the user will influence that perception. For example, an email system might:

- Display email messages by default either as a straightforward list, or as a list of 'threads' or conversations.

- Make it easy for users to send and receive messages from multiple email addresses by navigating through the main parts of the interface, or alternatively, make it possible to do this by changing various settings, or make it impossible by restricting users to using one email address only.

- Make it easy or difficult to choose from different email addresses for the same person, or see the email address associated with a person's name.

- Allow users to 'recall' messages they have sent within the same organisation, thus giving the impression that this is possible with email in general.

- Allow users to create an 'appointment' for a meeting with another user, sending an email notification and creating a diary entry simultaneously, thus giving the impression that these two different actions are a single action.

The options that the designers take will be informed by their understanding of what will be useful for the users, and will also shape the users' understanding of how email 'works'.

Finally, the **implementation model** is the model that the system architects and developers bring into being when turning the design into reality. For example, the implementation model underlying an email system is partly defined by the standards that specify how messages are processed using protocols such as POP3, IMAP and SMTP, and partly by the technical designers' approach to implementing these in software. This will include concepts that are alien to most users' mental models of email, such as ports and mailboxes, and might make no reference to user-oriented concepts such as message threads or email accounts.

Software designers and developers may document the implementation model using visual techniques such as class diagrams, state charts and interaction diagrams.

Not all conceptual and mental models are equal

The distinction between the terms 'conceptual model' and 'mental model' presented here follows the example of Johnson and Henderson (2002). In their language, 'conceptual model' refers to a design tool, a description created by the system's designer(s) of how it works. They stress that 'the conceptual model is *not the users' mental model* of the system'. It follows that the term 'mental model' should be reserved for talking about the user's model.

The terms are not always used in such a specific way. David Liddle (1996) talks about the 'user's conceptual model', which he defines as 'what the user is likely to think, and how the user is likely to respond'. Don Norman (1986) uses both 'conceptual model' and 'mental model' to denote the designer's model and the user's model equally. He distinguishes between them by using 'design model' and 'user's model' respectively, and refers to the perceptible aspects of the implemented system as the 'system image'.

As Don Norman (1986) describes, for a system to be usable there must be harmony between the user's mental model, the designers' conceptual model and the developers' implementation model. The product's user interface is the main lever available for the designers to ensure this is the case.

UX conceptual models are not data models

Business architects and analysts can find the idea of a conceptual model in UX hard to grasp. After all, isn't 'conceptual model' a very general term? Aren't data models, class models, data flow models, business process models and so on all different types of conceptual model? If this is your reaction, be aware that in UX the term is used with a specific, design-oriented meaning. Analysts' models are intended as representations of abstract information system elements (concepts) that the design must address. When designers talk about a 'concept', they are referring primarily to the design itself.

If your background includes enterprise architecture (EA), you will be familiar with an equally specific, but different, use of the term, to refer to a very high level data model. A UX conceptual model is not the same thing – an EA model is based on abstract business data concepts, whereas a UX model is oriented towards a creative idea in relation to users' thought processes.

That said, it is true that data modelling techniques such as entity modelling and Unified Modeling Language (UML) class models can be helpful tools when documenting a conceptual model.

AFFORDANCES

Information architecture is about making it obvious (or as obvious as possible) how to find what you want in a user interface. A key concept here is **affordance**.

Definition: affordance

The properties of an object that suggest to people how the object can be interacted with; the kind of interaction that is so suggested

In his landmark book *The Design of Everyday Things* (2013), Don Norman uses the example of door handles to demonstrate this. If we approach a door and see that it has no handle but only a smooth metal plate, we assume that we should not try to pull the door towards us, but push it using the metal plate. The door *affords* pushing; it does not afford pulling. Conversely, if we see a handle that affords gripping, we assume that we should pull rather than push.

This is crucial when designing user interfaces. For example, if it is possible to take an action by clicking on a web page element, such as a piece of text or an image, then the object should afford clicking. The object should look 'clicky'. This may mean that textual links should be underlined, for instance. We can extend the idea by saying that the object should not only afford clicking, but it should afford taking the kind of action that we want to take. This may mean using familiar icons or textual labels. Conversely, if a page element is currently disabled because it is irrelevant to the user's current task, it should be made unobtrusive so that it does not afford clicking, by using some technique such as 'greying out' (see the Delete Profile button in Figure 8.1 for example). It may be better to remove the element from the display altogether.

Conceptual models and affordances are closely related to the idea of metaphors in a user interface, which we discuss further in Chapter 9.

SUMMARY

In use, a system presents options and provides resources (functionality and content) to the user. It imposes requirements on the user to provide certain information and take certain actions in order to choose options and access resources. The system's designer must recognise what is being required of the user at each stage, take care that it is understandable, and ensure that what is being offered meets the user's needs.

There are several ways in which information in a user interface can be organised to support users' tasks. These can be remembered with the acronym LATCH – location, alphabet, time, category, hierarchy.

A good technique for finding out how to organise functionality or content is **card sorting**. An **open card sort** involves asking the users to group items into whatever categories they see fit and name the categories. A **closed card sort** asks the users to group items into predefined categories.

A system can be understood in terms of three different models, which should be in tune with each other for the system to be usable. The system's **conceptual model** is its structure and logical architecture as envisaged by the designer. The **mental model** is the version of it that is in the user's mind. The **implementation model** is the developers' view of the system, as may be represented in technical diagrams.

Elements of the user interface that are presented to the user need to make their purpose clear. An element's **affordances** are its properties that suggest to people how it can be interacted with.

REFERENCES

Johnson, J. and Henderson, A. (2002) Conceptual models: begin by designing what to design. *interactions*, 9(1), 25–32.

Liddle, D. (1996, April) Design of the conceptual model. In *Bringing Design to Software* (pp. 17–36). ACM, New York.

Norman, D.A. (1986) Cognitive engineering. In Norman, D.A. and Draper, S.W. (eds), *User Centered System Design: New Perspectives on Human-Computer Interaction*. Lawrence Erlbaum Associates, Hillsdale, NJ.

Norman, D.A. (2013) *The Design of Everyday Things: Revised and Expanded Edition*. Basic Books, New York.

Wurman, R.S. (2000) *Information Anxiety 2*. QUE, Indianapolis, IN.

FURTHER READING

Beyer, H. and Holtzblatt, K. (1997) *Contextual Design: Defining Customer-Centered Systems*. Morgan Kaufmann, San Francisco, CA.

Hudson, W. (2014) Card sorting. In Soegaard, M. and Dam, R.F. (eds), *The Encyclopedia of Human-Computer Interaction*. The Interaction Design Foundation, Aarhus, Denmark.

Krug, S. (2014) *Don't Make Me Think, Revisited*. New Riders, Berkeley, CA.

Redish, J.G. (2007) *Letting Go of the Words: Writing Web Content that Works*. Morgan Kaufmann, San Francisco, CA.

Rosenfeld, L., Morville, P. and Arango, J. (2015) *Information Architecture: For the Web and Beyond*. O'Reilly Media, Sebastopol, CA.

Spencer, D. (2009) *Card Sorting: Designing Usable Categories*. Rosenfeld Media, Brooklyn, NY.

EXAMPLE EXAMINATION QUESTIONS

1. **What might you analyse with monothetic agglomerative cluster analysis?**
   a. The distribution of task times in a usability test
   b. The transcripts from a contextual inquiry
   c. Participant ratings in a usability questionnaire
   d. The data from a card sorting session

2. Which of the following are accurate descriptions of card sorting?

1. With a closed card sort, participants aim to complete the activity within a fixed amount of time

2. With an open card sort, participants organise cards into groups that make sense to them

3. With a closed card sort, participants organise cards into predefined groups

4. With an open card sort, participants work in pairs to gain consensus on the group names

5. With a closed card sort, participants are drawn from a closed group of expert users

6. With an open card sort, participants can create as many or as few groups as they wish

    a.   2, 3 and 5 only

    b.   2, 3 and 6 only

    c.   1, 4 and 6 only

    d.   1, 4 and 5 only

3. What is 'affordance'?

a. The practice of creating strong lines that keep the viewer focused and cause user interface screens to look elegant

b. A question where the participant has to choose their answer from among a proposed list of responses. No answer other than the ones proposed is allowed

c. A visual design technique where the object of attention is made very different from the other elements that surround it

d. The properties of an object that suggest to people how the object can be interacted with

4. A website that sells organic food organises its produce by the area of the country from where the food originates. What organisational scheme is it using?

a. Time

b. Category

c. Location

d. Hierarchy

ANSWERS TO EXAMPLE QUESTIONS

1. The correct answer is (d).

This statistical technique is used to assign cases to groups (clusters) and so makes sense only for answer (d).

2. The correct answer is (b).

(1) is incorrect because participants do not work to a time limit. (4) is incorrect because participants do not work in pairs: you are after an individual's insights and you then get the 'consensus' through data analysis. (5) is a distracter that makes no sense: closed card sorts are not for expert users only. Option (b) is the only answer that has the three not discounted above.

3. The correct answer is (d).

All of the options are definitions such as those in the Glossary. The terms given are:

   a.   Alignment
   b.   A closed question
   c.   Contrast
   d.   Affordance

Thus option (d) is the required answer.

4. The correct answer is (c).

(c) is the correct choice because area of the country is a location-based scheme. (a) and (d) are wrong because area of the country has no relationship to time or hierarchy. It could only be a category scheme (option b) if it used a finite list of locations, but (c) is the best answer.

8 INTERACTION DESIGN

> Most people make the mistake of thinking design is what it looks like. People think it's this veneer – that the designers are handed this box and told, 'Make it look good!' That's not what we think design is. It's not just what it looks like and feels like. Design is how it works.
>
> Steve Jobs (quoted in Walker, 2003)

INTRODUCTION

This chapter is about designing user interfaces – not what they look like, but how they work. We define the concept of **interaction design** and set out basic principles for designing usable user interfaces. We give some examples of how to choose the right user interface controls when designing a graphical user interface (GUI). We introduce the idea of user interface patterns and present some examples of them. Finally, we discuss the importance of physical ergonomics and **Fitts' law**.

LEARNING OBJECTIVES

After reading this chapter you will be able to:

Remember	• Define the concept of progressive disclosure
	• State the difference between interaction design and information architecture
	• State the importance of focusing on the user's tasks when designing the flow of a user interface
Understand	• Describe different user interface design patterns
	• Describe how the choice of user interface control has an impact on the time it takes users to achieve their goals
	• Explain why user interface consistency is an important design principle
Apply	• Choose the correct interactive control in a user interface design

WHAT IS INTERACTION DESIGN?

Whereas information architecture is about helping users to find the content and functions that they need in order to carry out tasks, interaction design (IxD) is about what happens next: how does the user interact with the system to carry out the task?

Most often, tasks are initiated by the user themselves. With a digital product or service, this will typically involve the user choosing to access the application or site and carry out the task by interacting with the functionality which has been designed for that purpose. We also need to consider those interactions that are initiated by the system. For example, these might take the form of alerts using a mobile device's notifications functionality, or notifications via email or SMS.

Definition: interaction design

The practice of identifying design solutions and creating prototype user interfaces

Most digital products make use of the user's sense of sight to convey information and to show the possibilities that are available; for this reason, the next chapter is devoted to visual design. However, interaction design is not just about what things look like. Other modalities for interacting with digital products are becoming increasingly important. Systems often present information in auditory form, that is, via the user's sense of hearing. Assistive technology for people who cannot see usually falls into this category. Increasingly, systems take input from the user via speech. There are also interfaces that communicate via haptics, that is, the user's sense of touch: when your phone alerts you to a call by vibrating in your pocket, this is a haptic interface.

Interaction design involves addressing design issues in more abstract terms than simply what a screen display looks like. It is about designing the logic of the conversation that the user has with the system. This dialogue can then be implemented in different ways depending on the characteristics of both the user and the device they are using.

PRINCIPLES OF USABLE USER INTERFACES

Focus on the user's tasks: As we saw in Chapter 6, usability means effectiveness, efficiency and satisfaction in achieving goals. Therefore we have to *focus on the tasks* that the user must carry out to achieve their goals, and make it easy for them to carry them out quickly and accurately.

Keep it simple: When engaged in trying to complete a task, people only perceive what is relevant to that task. If an interface is designed without attention to this principle, and contains extraneous information or functionality, users will not perceive it. The importance of this point cannot be overstated. The *simpler* the interface, and the less clutter it contains, the easier it will be to understand and use. Respecting this principle in practice calls for constant vigilance on the part of the design team, to make sure that they are remembering 'You are not your user' (see Chapter 3). It is very hard for designers and developers, who are working with the product all day every day, to distance themselves from it sufficiently to take the user's point of view.

Be predictable: The interface will also be easier to understand and use if it is *consistent*: consistent with the user's experience of the rest of the system, and consistent with everything else in the user's experience of using comparable systems.

Leverage the user's knowledge: At the time of writing, it is still true to say that the designer of an interface based on speech and hearing, or an augmented reality application, may not be able to assume much of this experience on the user's part. However, when it comes to knowledge of how to use a visual interface, or GUI, the user is far from a blank slate. They will typically have invested thousands of hours using this operating system, or a similar one, and perhaps the same amount of time using similar applications. This has two implications for designing usable interfaces:

- *Exploit the user's knowledge of standard user interface controls* (by control, we mean elements that are employed by the user to take some action when operating a GUI, such as scrollbars, drop down menus, radio buttons, hyperlinks and so on). When you stop to think about it, the behaviour of some of these items is quite complex, but most users have already internalised this knowledge and know how to use the controls without thinking – *provided they are used in the appropriate context.*

- Conversely, *avoid inventing new user interface controls*, using standard ones in non-standard ways, or creating UI elements that look as if they are standard controls but in fact are not. This creates *cognitive friction* – the frustration that the user experiences when something does not work the way they expect it to.

Create accessibility using semantic markup: The common language that now forms the basis for thinking about interface design is Hypertext Markup Language (HTML). When we design a UI in terms of HTML elements, we are doing interaction design, not visual design, because HTML is a *semantic markup language*. In other words, the building blocks for the interface are not solely or primarily *visual* elements, even though we might think so when we see them displayed in a web browser. They are in fact instructions to the 'user agent' software (e.g. browser) about the *meaning* of each item on the page and how it relates to the other elements. This means that two different user agents can present the same interface in a completely different way, to support the varying needs of users with a range of abilities using a range of equipment. The difference might be relatively small, such as the use of different font sizes or background colours; or it might extend to using a completely different modality, such as input and output via speech instead of touchscreen or the classic GUI combination of keyboard, mouse and screen. This automatic translation from one interface style to another can only be reliably achieved if designers play by the rules.

CHOOSING THE RIGHT USER INTERFACE CONTROLS

Your choice of interface elements can have a significant impact on the time it takes users to achieve their goals. Consider the sequence of detailed cognitive and motor operations that the user has to go through in order to send a piece of information through a GUI:

- Find or remember the piece of information that is needed.

- Search the user interface for the relevant control.

- Recognise the type of control, remember how it is used and understand the constraints it places on the information that can be entered – or otherwise work it out by trial and error.

- Position themselves correctly in relation to the input device.

- Interact with the input device so as to enter the information.

- Recognise whether they have entered the information as intended.
- If an error condition is signalled by the system, recognise that this has happened, understand what the problem is and start again.

At each step of the way, the difference between a correct or incorrect choice of control is potentially huge in terms of effectiveness, efficiency and satisfaction. These general principles will help when selecting user interface controls:

- Use a control that the user expects to encounter.
- Make it hard, or preferably impossible, to submit invalid information.
- Avoid hiding information that is likely to help orientate the user.
- Conversely, do hide information that is unlikely to be helpful.
- Prioritise usability on the device that the user is most likely to be using.

Below are some guidelines for putting these principles into practice and using GUI controls appropriately in particular situations. These are a starting point. If you have a good reason to believe that 'best practice' may not give your users the best results in a particular case, you should test your hypothesis by incorporating some relevant testing into your user research schedule.

Moving to another page

Use a *hyperlink*. Another option is a *button*, but a button implies the intention to take a specific action rather than simply navigate elsewhere. It is possible to apply visual styling to a hyperlink so that it looks exactly like a button (or vice versa), but be aware that the options are not treated the same way by all devices or by assistive technology.

Choosing only one of two options

Use a pair of *radio buttons*. Do not use checkboxes. An alternative is to use a *toggle* control, but there are two potential drawbacks with this:

- Toggle controls are not directly supported by some UI languages, such as HTML, so will not work so reliably across devices or with assistive technology.
- Because there are only two options in a toggle control, it is easy to design it in a confusing way so that it is hard for the user to know whether it is on or off.

Figure 8.1 shows an example of this kind of two-part control: a segmented control containing two options, 'Display' and 'Color'. Which one is currently active? The user might imagine the answer to be 'Display', since the text underneath begins with that word. However, the correct answer is that 'Color' is currently active.

Choosing one or two of two options

Use a pair of *checkboxes*. Do not use radio buttons.

Figure 8.1 Two-part control

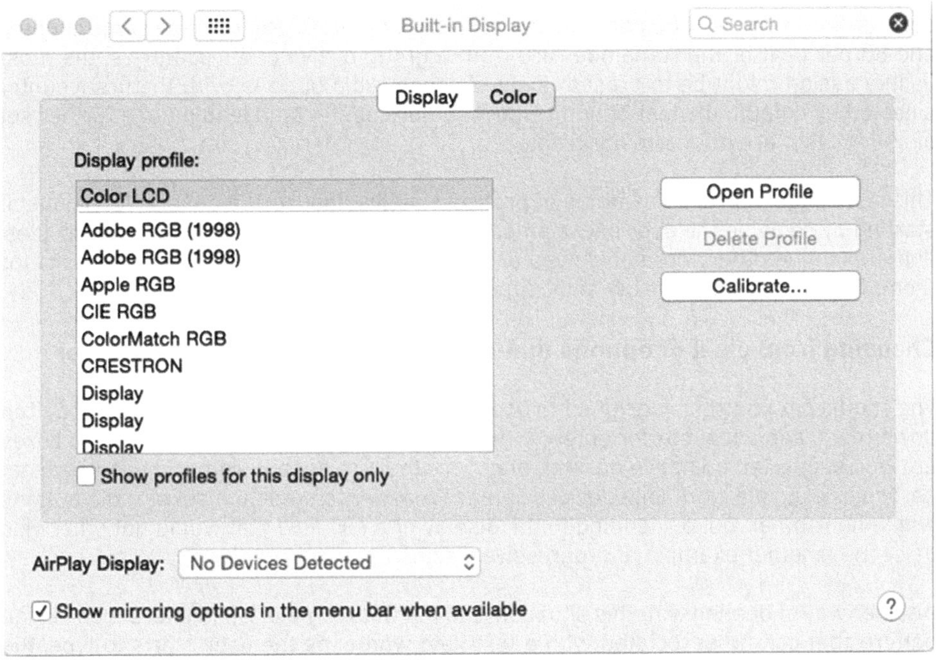

Choosing from a fixed set of three or more options

There are two questions to ask in this situation:

- Are the options mutually exclusive?
- Can all the options be displayed simultaneously?

If the options are not mutually exclusive, use a set of *checkboxes*. Do not use radio buttons. Another option is a *list box* (see the list of profiles in Figure 8.1 for example). The drawbacks of a list box are:

- They are relatively uncommon, so some people do not know how to use them – for example, by using the Control and Shift keys correctly in Microsoft Windows.
- In HTML, list boxes are implemented using the <select> element, which can be hard to use on mobile devices.

If the options are mutually exclusive, use a set of *radio buttons*. Do not use checkboxes.

Sometimes the number of possible options is very large. For example, a list of countries might have more than 200 entries. In this case, a set of radio buttons will take up so much space on the screen that the user will be obliged to scroll to see it all, and will not be able to see the rest of the display at the same time. The *dropdown list* control is designed for presenting lists without taking up extra space on the screen, and is very widely used, both for this reason and because it is easy to implement. However, it is one of the least usable controls, precisely because the options are hidden most of the time. A better approach might be to consider whether it is always necessary to show all the options. For example, if 80 per cent of your website visitors are from the same country, and 80 per cent of the remainder are from a group of five other countries, the most usable design might be to present a set of seven radio buttons, with the first country selected by default, the last option being 'Another country' and leading to a further set of options that are not normally visible.

This last suggestion is an example of **progressive disclosure**, the general technique of starting by showing the user only a small set of information or interaction possibilities, and presenting other, more advanced or obscure options if the user explicitly asks for them. This reduces complexity and clutter in the UI.

Choosing from a set of options that may not contain the desired answer

The *combo box* control is designed to deal with this situation – a combination of a drop down menu and a text box for entering the answer if absent from the list. Combo boxes are well supported on native desktop platforms, but are absent from HTML and are not particularly usable on mobile devices. It may be better to present a set of radio buttons with a final 'other' option, leading to the display of a *text field* that would not otherwise be seen – another example of progressive disclosure.

Another way of dealing with this situation is to use *auto complete* – an interaction design pattern that can be associated with a text field where, as the user starts to type, the system displays a list of matching suggestions that can be picked from.

Entering a structured piece of information

When entering a structured piece of information such as a date, URL, telephone number, email address or credit card number, think carefully about the users' characteristics, the task context and the technical environment when deciding how to support these operations, and in critical cases, consider doing usability testing. HTML5 provides special-purpose form elements for the first four examples listed. (Note that at the time of writing, there are deficiencies in support for the `<input type="number">` HTML5 element in some browsers and assistive technology.) These make it easier for the user to enter the right information and avoid errors. For example, if an input control is designated as a telephone number, a touchscreen device should display a numeric keypad so that the user does not enter non-numeric characters in the field. However, remember that platform support for HTML5 varies widely.

Date picker controls make it impossible to enter an invalid date. However, they can be hard to use if they force the user to scroll repeatedly. Choose a default value that minimises scrolling. It may sometimes be preferable to use simple numeric input fields for the year, month and day. A form sometimes contains multiple date fields with logical interdependencies, for example, the start and end date for a booking. Usability testing should find any problems resulting from the way you have designed for this situation.

USER INTERFACE PATTERNS

The palette of elements that can be used to make up a user interface ranges from the large-scale to the detailed. The controls discussed above are at the level of fine detail. Conventional ways of structuring user interaction at a higher level are often referred to as *patterns*. Design patterns are collected and documented in many books (for example, Scott and Neil, 2009) and websites. Each pattern exists to solve a specific type of generic design problem. As with form controls, using well-established patterns in a predictable way is an excellent technique for leveraging your users' existing knowledge and experience, as well as the effort that other designers have put into developing and refining these ideas. It is beyond the scope of this book to catalogue patterns extensively, but a few examples are discussed below to give you a flavour of their nature and scope.

Faceted search

Problem: The user wants to find a list of items that meet various different criteria simultaneously. The required flexibility cannot be achieved with a single hierarchical information architecture optimised for one browsing strategy.

Solution: Provide a set of search controls that allow the user to experiment with specifying and changing criteria under several different headings (facets) at the same time (see Figure 8.2).

Figure 8.2 Clothes shopping with faceted search

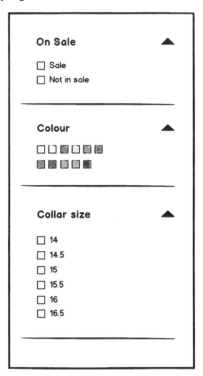

Pagination

Problem: The user of a web application wants to see a list of information items. However, there may be hundreds, thousands or even millions of items that match the search criteria. Putting all this information on one page would seriously damage performance and overwhelm the user.

Solution: Split the results into subsets of, say, 50 items at a time and display each subset on a different page. Provide controls that allow the user to go forwards and backwards through the sequence of pages, or jump to the beginning or the end (see Figure 8.3). Tell the user how many pages there are in total, and what the number of the page they are currently looking at is. Optionally, provide links allowing the user to go straight to any one of the next few pages. Optionally, allow them to type in the number of a page to go straight there. Optionally, allow the user to change the number of items on each page.

Figure 8.3 Pagination control

《 Previous Page   1 2 3 ... 26   Next Page 》

Infinite scrolling

Problem: The same problem as addressed by the Pagination control.

Solution: Whenever the user scrolls down to the end of the page, automatically display additional results without the user needing to take any action, so that the amount of information on the page grows progressively.

Breadcrumbs

Problem: A website has an information architecture several layers deep. To stay orientated within the overall structure, the user needs help in remembering the path that they have followed to reach the current page from the home page, and may like to be able to reach any of the intermediate pages easily.

Solution: At the top of each page, present a chain of links representing the sequence of pages that the user followed to reach this page from the home page (Figure 8.4).

Figure 8.4 Breadcrumbs (Source: https://www.w3schools.com/howto/tryit. asp?filename=tryhow_css_breadcrumbs)

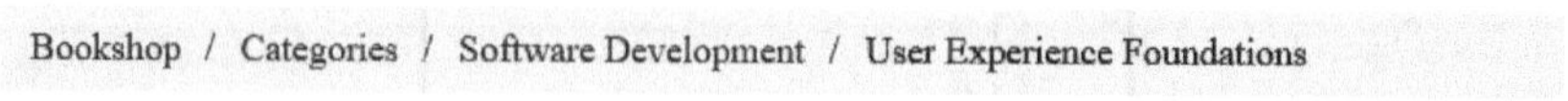

Bookshop / Categories / Software Development / User Experience Foundations

Wizard

Problem: To carry out a particular task, such as setting up an application for the first time, making a purchase or signing up for a service, it is necessary for the user of the product to carry out a large number of steps – more than can be done reasonably on one page. There may be multiple possible paths through the process. If the user abandons it part-way through, the application will be left in an inconsistent state, so their changes will need to be discarded.

Solution: Organise the process into a predictable sequence of steps split up into a series of pages, supporting the multiple possibilities in as simple and quick a way as possible. Guide the user through the sequence, making it hard for them to get distracted from the task in hand by removing other navigation items for the duration of the task. Give a clear visual indication of how many steps there are in the process, and how many have been carried out so far.

Organiser-Workspace

Problem: The user needs to navigate around a database of items or documents, organised into folders. They need to see a list of all the items within a folder, while also maintaining an overview of the folder structure and their current place in it. Having chosen an item to examine more closely, or decided to create a new one, they then need to be able to work on it in detail.

Solution: Divide the screen into left and right. In the left-hand pane, show a hierarchical tree browser control, allowing the user to navigate around the folder structure, focus on areas of interest by expanding and collapsing branches of the tree, and select one folder for examination. Divide the right-hand pane into top and bottom. In the top pane, show a list of the items in the selected folder, with columns showing attributes of each item. Use the bottom pane as a workspace for viewing and editing an individual item. Preferably, allow the user to resize the panes by moving the boundaries between them. This is what Alan Cooper et al. (2014) call the Organiser-Workspace pattern, and has been typical for Microsoft products for many years (see Figure 8.5).

Figure 8.5 The Organiser-Workspace pattern

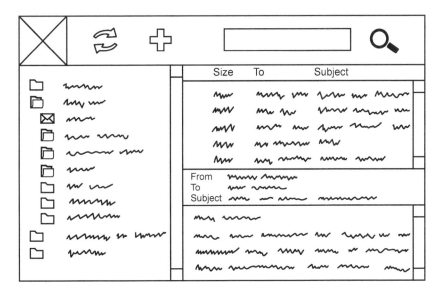

Carousel

Problem: The user wants to choose from a set of items that are best represented by pictures. If the screen is large, showing all the pictures on the screen might be possible, but would be overwhelming and would make it hard to find the right item (see Hick's law). If the screen is small, it is only possible to show one picture at a time anyway.

Solution: Show one picture (or, if space permits, a small number of pictures arranged in a horizontal row) at a time, with controls to the left and right of the picture to indicate that other pictures are available to be browsed through, and make it possible to scroll left or right as easily as possible, by swiping, using the keyboard's arrow keys or clicking on the screen to either side of the currently displayed picture. Optionally, the pictures could be programmed to scroll automatically every second or two in the absence of user interaction (however, note that animating the UI in a way that diminishes the user's control over it is generally not a good idea). A common convention is to show the number of items in the carousel with a number of small circles underneath it, one of which has its appearance altered to show that it is the currently visible one.

PHYSICAL ERGONOMICS OF USER INTERFACE CONTROLS

The design of user interface controls is largely a matter of cognitive ergonomics: how can we optimise the product to fit the user's mental processes? However, operating a user interface also calls for physical, as well as cognitive effort. The user needs to be physically able to see the controls and manipulate them using parts of their body, such as their hand to operate a mouse, or their fingertips to use a touchscreen.

On touchscreens, controls need to be large enough and have enough space around them for the user to be able to touch the right area without accidentally touching something else. This includes people with large fingers, people whose hands are shaking and those with long fingernails.

Using a mouse or trackpad is hard for many people, either because of motor disability or as a result of working in a cramped space or with an unfamiliar computer. Even for those with no such difficulties, moving the mouse pointer a long distance on the screen requires moving the mouse a long way. The operation is even harder if the control being moved to is small. The larger the controls and the smaller the required mouse movements, the more efficiently the user will be able to carry out their tasks. Fitts' law states this in more formal terms.

Fitts' law

The time taken to move to a target is a function of the target size and the distance to the target.

For people who find a mouse difficult, particularly severe problems are presented by controls that require a combination of moving the mouse, waiting for visual feedback and holding down or releasing the mouse button. Examples of this are dragging an icon into a folder and waiting for the folder to be highlighted before releasing the mouse button, or using a multi-level drop down menu where the user has to move the mouse pointer over the right toolbar menu item in order see the drop down menu, then move the mouse pointer over the right item in the menu to see the next level of the menu, and so on, all without accidentally moving the mouse off the menu so that it disappears and they have to start again.

SUMMARY

Interaction design involves thinking about the flow of information between user and system at a detailed level. Without committing prematurely to any decisions about visual form, the interaction designer designs prototype interface mechanisms that allow the team to test out ideas for how the user can most effectively carry out their tasks.

Useful and usable interfaces are simple, focused on the user's tasks, take into account the user's knowledge and expectations, and are designed from the beginning to be usable on a range of devices that are appropriate for the users. Choosing suitable interface mechanisms can have a strong positive or negative effect on effectiveness, efficiency and satisfaction.

The choice of interactive controls is partly a matter of using well-established tools in the correct fashion. Another way of leveraging the user's existing knowledge and avoiding the creation of baffling homemade solutions is to take advantage of well-documented and familiar user interface patterns, such as wizards, Organiser-Workspace, breadcrumbs and faceted search.

REFERENCES

Cooper, A., Reimann, R., Cronin, D. and Noessel, C. (2014) *About Face: The Essentials of Interaction Design*. Wiley, Indianapolis, IN.

Scott, B. and Neil, T. (2009) *Designing Web Interfaces: Principles and Patterns for Rich Interactions*. O'Reilly Media, Sebastopol, CA.

Walker, R. (2003) The guts of a new machine. *The New York Times*, 30.

FURTHER READING

Goodwin, K. (2011) *Designing for the Digital Age: How to Create Human-Centered Products and Services*. Wiley, Indianapolis, IN.

Jarrett, C. and Gaffney, G. (2008) *Forms That Work: Designing Web Forms for Usability*. Morgan Kaufmann, Burlington, MA.

EXAMPLE EXAMINATION QUESTIONS

1. You are creating a form for a hotel booking system. One field is titled, 'Select a type of room' and the possible answers are 'Single', 'Double' and 'Twin'. What would be the correct user interface control to accept responses?

   a. A set of radio buttons

   b. A set of checkboxes

   c. A free text field

   d. A drop down menu

2. Users are requested to indicate at the end of the online application which daily newspaper(s) they read. Which would be the MOST appropriate user interface control to use?

   a. Check boxes

   b. Radio buttons

   c. Text box

   d. Drop down menu

3. Which law states that the time required to move to a target is a function of the target size and distance to the target?

   a. Hick's law

   b. The power law of practice

   c. Fitts' law

   d. Nielsen's law

4. The design team are struggling to decide whether to use a set of radio buttons or a drop down menu to help users choose from a list of about 12 items. What would you advise?

   a. Choose a drop down menu as this will reduce the amount of screen real estate needed for the control

   b. Choose radio buttons as this will expose all of the options to users without them having to click to see the choices

   c. Prototype both alternatives and observe how users interact with the controls in an upcoming usability test

   d. Design a new control that combines the best of both approaches

ANSWERS TO EXAMPLE QUESTIONS

1. The correct answer is (a).

(b) is incorrect because this will accept more than one choice and the choices are mutually exclusive ('Choose a type of room'). (c) is incorrect because it will result in typing errors. (d) is incorrect because there are only three choices and using a drop down is less efficient than clicking a single radio button (click to activate the drop down, scroll to correct answer, release mouse). This leaves (a) as the correct answer.

2. The correct answer is (a).

The question indicates that more than one choice can be made. This rules out radio buttons and a drop down menu for selection. Entering text into a free format text box allows all kinds of difficulties to be encountered – is 'The Times' the same as 'Times'? And what about 'The London Times'? Having eliminated other choices, the best option is that which remains, option (a) – check boxes.

3. The correct answer is (c).

(a) is wrong because Hick's law refers to the time taken to make a decision with a user interface based on the number of choices. (b) is wrong because this refers to learning improvement with time. (d) is wrong because Nielsen's law refers to internet bandwidth. This leaves (c) as the correct answer.

4. The correct answer is (c).

The purpose of this question is to see if candidates realise that the best way to choose between options in a user interface is by having real user data rather than opinions. (d) is wrong, because it makes sense to use a control that's consistent with other controls that people use, rather than create a new one. Without any more information about the context in the question stem, it's impossible to choose between (a) and (b) since both might be sensible choices in a particular context. This leaves (c) as the correct choice. Although it's true that it might not make sense to run a usability test if the only aim of the test was to make a decision about controls, the question points out that this is an 'upcoming' test, so it would be a quick and cheap way to inject this question into the upcoming test and get a definitive answer.

9   VISUAL DESIGN

> What a thing is and what it means are not separate ... The perception of what a thing is and the perception of what it means are not separate, either.
>
> James J. Gibson (1982)

INTRODUCTION

In previous chapters, we have stressed the importance of avoiding premature commitment to visual details when sketching and prototyping interfaces. Yet there comes a point in the development of any interface where visual design inevitably becomes the focus of attention.

Visual design is a specialist skill, which takes years of training and practice to acquire to a professional level. A thorough mastery of it is a very long way beyond the scope of this book. However, we can at least introduce some of the basic concepts that underpin visual designers' work, and which can potentially be used by anyone to improve the layout of an interface in a simple way. In this chapter we examine the ideas of **proximity, alignment, repetition** and **contrast**. We discuss the use of *metaphors* in visual design. Finally, we consider the place of **eye-tracking** techniques in evaluating visual design, and introduce some of the key terminology.

LEARNING OBJECTIVES

After reading this chapter you will be able to:

Remember	• List fundamental principles of visual design
	• Define eye tracking as a research method and recall key insights from eye-tracking research
Understand	• Identify good and poor page layouts
	• Describe the advantages and disadvantages of using metaphorical representations in visual design

WHAT IS VISUAL DESIGN?

As we discussed in Chapter 3, the term 'design' is used in a variety of senses, and even 'visual design' suffers from the same problem. For this reason, the syllabus for the BCS Foundation Certificate in User Experience adopts a very specific definition listing four elements:

Definition: visual design

The practice of devising grids, laying out pages, choosing colour palettes and developing icons

The syllabus includes some details about the first two items, but not the last two. For more information on all these topics, see Williams (2014) and some of the more specialised texts referenced in the 'Further reading' section at the end of this chapter. A related subject, not explicitly mentioned in the definition, is typography – the art of choosing or designing typefaces – which is also covered by Williams (2014) and others.

To the non-specialist, visual design can seem a mysterious craft – 'creative' and therefore somehow not governed by the same sort of rational calculations that we have described elsewhere. It is important to remember that one of the key goals of the visual designer is, or should be, the same as that of the interaction designer: to help the user to find, understand, remember and use the resources offered by the system.

PRINCIPLES OF LAYOUT AND FORMATTING

Robin Williams (2014) describes four principles of layout and formatting, which are effective and universally applicable because they are fundamentally rooted in the way that human beings perceive things. They are proximity, alignment, repetition and contrast.

PARC

The four basic principles of layout and formatting can be remembered using the mnemonic PARC:

P proximity
A alignment
R repetition
C contrast

PARC also happens to stand for the Palo Alto Research Center, where the GUI was invented. Other memorable arrangements of the same four letters are possible – for example, CARP.

Proximity

Proximity is about things being close to each other. When we see things located close together, we perceive them as a group and tend to assume, rightly or wrongly, that they are related to each other. When things are not close together, we assume that they are not connected. We can exploit this feature of human perception when designing an interface. Grouping related items together and putting plenty of *negative space* between unrelated groups of things makes it easier for the user to see the relationships and discern the inherent structure of the information. Following this principle should result in a screen with a handful of clearly separate groups of information. This makes it more likely that the user will find the information they need and remember it.

A common mistake of inexperienced designers is to leave insufficient negative space on the page, which makes the groupings of content less evident.

Alignment

We see the alignment principle at work every time we read a newspaper or a book. Every item on the page should be placed in such a way that at least one of its edges is aligned with other elements on the page. For example, each paragraph on this page is aligned with the other paragraphs along both its left and its right edges. This creates a strong sense of clarity and organisation. It allows the reader to focus on the meaning of the words, rather than on trying to find a visual structure. If a layout has no apparent structure, a portion of our mental energy will be dissipated uselessly in trying to find one.

When a screen has been organised with attention to this principle, invisible but nevertheless very clear lines demarcating the areas of content will be apparent to the user. In fact, designers lay out pages with these lines, as defined by *grid systems*.

Another common 'rookie error' is to over-use centred text. A centred layout has no clear alignment. This makes the content harder to read and understand.

Repetition

Whereas alignment creates harmony by organising the edges of items on the screen in an orderly way, repetition creates unifying threads or motifs that run through the entire visual design. If you look at any well-designed website you will see many examples of repetition, for example:

- The headings and subheadings use a consistent typeface and font size.
- The normal text uses a consistent typeface and font size.
- Margins around individual items and around the main display are a consistent width.
- A small set of colours is used consistently.
- 'Glyphs' or small images that form part of the text formatting (such as the bullet points in this list) all look the same.
- Lists of items use the same format for each separate item, whether it is a short word or phrase in a navigation control, or a relatively complicated item with its own internal structure, perhaps including an image, a subheading and so on.

Contrast

Contrast makes a display interesting and attractive, unlike the dull and unappealing interfaces that the users of desktop software were used to for many years. Contrast is achieved, for example, by using headings and subheadings that are not just slightly larger than normal text, but much larger and a different colour; or by having areas of the screen that invert the colour scheme so that the foreground and background colours are reversed.

A third common mistake of inexperienced designers is to be too timid about the contrast between the size of headings and the size of normal text. As Williams (2014) says, 'If two items are not exactly the same, then make them different. Really different.'

VISUAL METAPHORS

An important part of designing a system's conceptual model (see Chapter 7) is the selection of one or more appropriate *metaphors* for the system. A metaphor helps the user to understand a system by using concepts that they can easily relate to. The metaphor may be based directly on objects in the task domain, or alternatively it may simply be chosen because it provides a strong, unifying idea that is well suited to modelling the task domain. For example, an ecommerce website may use the metaphor of a shop, or a workflow system may use terms relating to an assembly line.

Sometimes a metaphor is effective even though it does not seem to provide a very good mapping of the task domain. For example, the best-known metaphor to many computer users is the 'desktop' metaphor, which conjures up a physical desktop that includes such unlikely ideas as folders within folders, a trash can or waste bin that sits on the desktop, and windows that can appear and disappear on top of it. Conversely, following a real-world metaphor too closely can undermine its effectiveness and try the user's patience. The best metaphors sometimes take a single idea from the real physical world, such as a pin-board in Pinterest, but do not treat it too literally.

Similar considerations apply when we think about the visual representation of concepts in the system. A visual metaphor can be a helpful way of making information easier to see and understand. Icons are an example of this, provided that they are used to supplement textual labels rather than to replace them. The power of an icon is a function of its distinctiveness and familiarity, rather than its direct relevance to the topic. Many common icons are stylised versions of physical objects in an old-fashioned or obsolete form, such as a floppy disk icon for the 'Save' function.

When designing an interface for use by an international audience, it is tempting to sidestep language translation issues by using icons instead of textual labels. An example of this can be seen in the iconography used at airports, for example. However, caution is needed. Icons do not always translate well across cultures. For example, a 'thumbs-up' indicates approval to a British or American person, but is an offensive gesture in some cultures.

Too much metaphor

When a real-world object is being used as a visual metaphor, its physical attributes should not be slavishly reproduced on a digital display. This is known as *skeuomorphism*, and can be seen, for example, in Apple's iOS6, where some applications carefully mimic the grain of a wooden bookshelf or the stitching in a leather-bound notebook. These details are distracting and clutter the user interface for no good reason. A computer is a computer, after all, and digital displays should not pretend to be something else.

EYE TRACKING

Although using the layout and formatting principles discussed above will go some way towards making sure that the user can locate the information that they need without too much trouble, sometimes we need experimental data that will tell us exactly how well our layout supports the user's needs. To do this, the best approach is often to use a straightforward task-based evaluation as described in Chapter 11. To give an extra level of empirical data, we can carry out **eye-tracking**, which uses special-purpose equipment to measure where the user is looking at any given moment, and where they look next.

Only a very small area in the centre of our visual field allows us to see clearly, with so-called *foveal vision*. This means that, although we are not usually aware of it, we move our eyes quite often, typically three to four times a second, in order to focus on different things. These small movements are called **saccades**. Eye-tracking equipment directs infrared light at a user's eyes and measures the reflection of it from different parts of the eye to determine exactly where they are looking – the *point of gaze* – and to identify the saccades that occur.

In a UX context, there are two types of output that are commonly derived from an eye-tracking experiment. The first is a **gaze plot** as shown in Figure 9.1, which shows what is displayed on the screen and superimposes on it a representation of the different points of gaze recorded during one user's session with the interface.

The second type of output is a **heat map**, as shown in Figure 9.2. This can show findings from a single user or an aggregation of all the findings from many users, and shows us which parts of the display were looked at for the longest time.

Gaze plots and heat maps can give us valuable information about parts of a layout that attract, or fail to attract, the user's attention at appropriate or inappropriate moments. One well-known general finding from eye-tracking research (Nielsen, 2006) tells us that visitors to a web page tend to look at it in an F-shaped pattern. First, they read across the top of the main content (not the page header). Then their gaze shifts down a little and again goes from left to right, but this time not so far across. Finally, they scan vertically down the left-hand side of the page content. These three movements make the shape of a capital F. In response to this, not only should we place important information in the first two paragraphs of a page, but key words should be right at the beginning of the sentences that start those paragraphs.

Figure 9.1 Gaze plot (Image courtesy of Tobii AB)

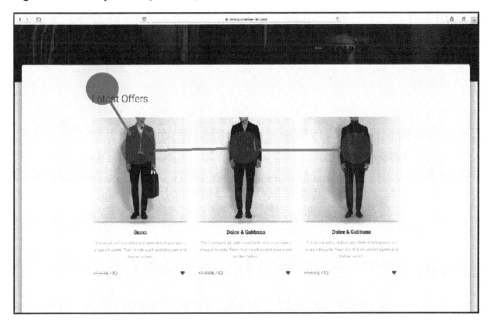

Figure 9.2 Heat map (Image courtesy of Tobii AB)

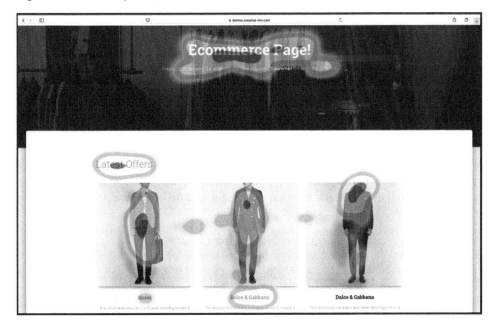

It is likely that the F pattern has its basis in the reading order naturally imposed by languages such as English, which are read from top to bottom and from left to right. Consequently, it is particularly relevant when the page's content is mainly textual. Some research (e.g. Djamasbi et al., 2011) suggests that where images form the main part of the content, readers can be encouraged to make better use of the whole screen by distributing images evenly over its area. A similar effect may be achieved with text by formatting it into self-contained boxes spread across the screen. Other findings include the following:

- *Long paragraphs* are often not read, wherever they are placed.
- *Images* tend to divert the viewer's attention away from text.
- Photographs of *people's faces* attract attention particularly strongly.
- However, content (especially images) that the reader judges to be an *advertisement* will usually be ignored – this is referred to as *banner blindness*.
- Text and other content that is *not relevant* to the user's immediate goal will tend not to be noticed.

SUMMARY

Visual design is about devising grids, laying out pages, choosing colour palettes and developing icons.

The layout of any page, in terms of the user's ability to perceive its structure and content, can potentially be improved by using the elements of the mnemonic PARC:

- Proximity: group related items together and put plenty of space between unrelated groups of things.
- Alignment: line up the edges of text blocks, images and other content, particularly at the top and left.
- Repetition: make things look the same as each other, so that any differences can be seen more clearly.
- Contrast: when two items serve a different purpose, make them look clearly distinct from each other.

A metaphor based on a simple, real-world idea like a desktop or a playlist can make an interface easier to grasp by providing a powerful unifying concept. Metaphors work best when they are not overdone. Icons need to be clear and distinctive rather than realistic, and can be subject to culture-specific interpretation.

We can get accurate data on exactly where test participants are looking at any one time by using eye tracking. A user can only look at one small area at a time – this is the *point of gaze*. The small involuntary movements of the eye from one point of gaze to another are called *saccades*. A *gaze plot* shows the sequence of these eye movements during a user's session. A *heat map* can show the areas of the page that attracted users' attention for the longest periods. A website user's typical approach to reading a page of text is to read the top few rows and then down the left-hand site in an *F pattern*.

REFERENCES

Djamasbi, S., Siegel, M. and Tullis, T. (2011) Visual hierarchy and viewing behavior: An eye tracking study. In *International Conference on Human-Computer Interaction* (pp. 331-340). Springer, Berlin, Heidelberg.

Gibson, J.J. (1982) The affordances of the environment. In Reed, E.S. and Jones, R. (eds), *Reasons for Realism: Selected Essays of James J. Gibson*. Lawrence Erlbaum Associates, Inc, Hillsdale, NJ.

Nielsen, J. (2006) *F-Shaped Pattern for Reading Web Content*. Nielsen Norman Group, Fremont, CA.

Pernice, K. (2017) *F-Shaped Pattern of Reading on the Web: Misunderstood, But Still Relevant (Even on Mobile)*. Nielsen Norman Group. Available from: https://www.nngroup.com/articles/f-shaped-pattern-reading-web-content/

Williams, R. (2014) *The Non-Designer's Design Book: Design and Typographic Principles for the Visual Novice*. Pearson Education, San Francisco.

FURTHER READING

Albers, J. (2013) *Interaction of Color*. Yale University Press, New Haven, CT.

Bergstrom, J.R. and Schall, A. (eds) (2014) *Eye Tracking in User Experience Design*. Elsevier, Waltham, MA.

Bojko, A. (2013) *Eye Tracking the User Experience: A Practical Guide to Research*. Rosenfeld Media, Brooklyn, NY.

Golombisky, K. and Hagen, R. (2013) *White Space Is Not Your Enemy: A Beginner's Guide to Communicating Visually through Graphic, Web & Multimedia Design*. Taylor & Francis, Burlington, MA.

Jarrett, C. and Gaffney, G. (2008) *Forms That Work: Designing Web Forms for Usability*. Morgan Kaufmann, Burlington, MA.

Leborg, C. (2006) *Visual Grammar*. Princeton Architectural Press, New York.

Lidwell, W., Holden, K. and Butler, J. (2010) *Universal Principles of Design, Revised and Updated: 125 Ways to Enhance Usability, Influence Perception, Increase Appeal, Make Better Design Decisions, and Teach through Design*. Rockport Publishers, Beverly, MA.

Lupton, E. (2014) *Thinking with Type: A Critical Guide for Designers, Writers, Editors, & Students*. Chronicle Books, San Francisco, CA.

Lynch, P.J. (2008) *Web Style Guide*. Yale University Press, New Haven, CT.

Mullet, K. and Sano, D. (1995) *Designing Visual Interfaces: Communication Oriented Techniques*. Prentice-Hall, Inc, Englewood Cliffs, NJ.

Tufte, E. (1983) *The Visual Display of Quantitative Information*. Graphics Press, Cheshire, CT.

Wroblewski, L. (2008) *Web Form Design: Filling in the Blanks*. Rosenfeld Media, Brooklyn, NY.

EXAMPLE EXAMINATION QUESTIONS

1. In a usability study, a researcher needs to understand where the user's point of gaze is directed while completing an on-screen form. Which technique is MOST appropriate?

   a. A retrospective protocol

   b. A/B testing

   c. Eye tracking

   d. A summative usability test

2. Eye-tracking research shows that users' gaze patterns when reading web content tend to form what kind of shape?

   a. An L shape

   b. An F shape

   c. A W shape

   d. A C shape

3. The practice of creating strong lines that keep the viewer focused and cause the page to look elegant exploits which principle of visual design?

   a. Contrast

   b. Repetition

   c. Proximity

   d. Alignment

4. Match the following terms to their definitions.

   1. Saccade

   2. Gaze plot

   3. Heat map

   4. Fixation

   W. A representation of the different areas of the screen where the user has spent the most time looking

   X. A pause of the eye movement on a specific area of the visual field

   Y. A moment-by-moment representation of a user's eye movement across the screen

   Z. Rapid eye movements

      a. 1X, 2W, 3Y, 4Z

      b. 1X, 2Y, 3W, 4Z

      c. 1Z, 2Y, 3W, 4X

      d. 1Z, 2W, 3Y, 4X

ANSWERS TO EXAMPLE QUESTIONS

1. The correct answer is (c).

(a) is sometimes used in combination with eye tracking to understand why the user was looking in a particular place, but on its own it will not provide the answer the researcher needs. (b) is the wrong answer because A/B testing is a technique used to compare two alternative designs with a large number of users and provides no details on eye tracking. (d) is the wrong answer because a summative usability test is used to measure effectiveness, efficiency and satisfaction and provides no details on eye tracking. This leaves (c) as the correct answer.

2. The correct answer is (b).

The evidence for the F shape is from Pernice (2017). Although it doesn't form a perfect 'F', it certainly doesn't look like a W, L or C. So option (b) is the correct answer.

3. The correct answer is (d).

(a) is wrong: the purpose of contrast is to organise the screen and make it more interesting. (b) is wrong because the purpose of repetition is to create consistency and to add visual interest. (c) is wrong because the purpose of proximity is to organise and group the various parts of the UI. This leaves (d) as the correct answer.

4. The correct answer is (c).

These terms are clearly defined in the eye-tracking literature but students sometimes confuse 'fixation' with 'saccade' and 'gaze plot' with 'heat map' so the answers have been carefully ordered to test for this confusion. (c) is the only correct answer.

10 USER INTERFACE PROTOTYPING

The architect's two most important tools are: the eraser in the drafting room and the wrecking bar on the site.

Frank Lloyd Wright (quoted in Jacobs, 1965)

INTRODUCTION

In previous chapters, we have repeatedly mentioned the importance of prototyping: it is an essential part of the iterative user-centred design process. In this chapter we describe exactly what we mean by a prototype. We examine the different sorts of **prototype**, such as electronic and paper prototypes, and we identify the difference between a prototype and a **sketch**. We also clarify the term **wireframe**. We discuss the applicability of different sorts of prototype in different situations.

LEARNING OBJECTIVES

After reading this chapter you will be able to:

Understand	• Recognise the appropriate type of prototype for the phase of design
	• Describe the differences between prototypes and sketches
	• Recognise the importance of identifying multiple design solutions before deciding on a specific design solution
Apply	• Choose between different types of prototype, for example paper and electronic, and recall the merits of each
	• Sketch paper prototypes

WHAT IS A PROTOTYPE?

Definition: prototype

Representation of all or part of an interactive system, that, although limited in some way, can be used for analysis, design and evaluation (ISO 9241-210, 2019)

People sometimes use the word 'prototype' in a restricted sense: for example, to indicate only representations that are created using electronic technology, as opposed to *mockups*, that can be paper-based; or to include only *evolutionary* prototypes as opposed to *throwaway* prototypes (see below). In this book, we follow the ISO 9241-210 definition, given above, which is very broad and encompasses all types of representation created for the purpose of analysis, design and evaluation. This includes:

- Interactive electronic prototypes and paper prototypes
- Evolutionary and throwaway prototypes
- Horizontal and vertical prototypes
- High-fidelity and low-fidelity prototypes
- Mockups
- Wireframes

The one distinction we do make is between prototypes and sketches.

Sketches

A sketch is not a prototype!

Sketching is an essential part of what designers do. It is a way of developing ideas, which has been described as 'thinking with a pencil'. A sketch is not suitable for using as a prototype. A prototype needs to be something that the user can understand and interact with in some way.

Although we do refer to the activity of drawing a paper-based prototype by hand as 'sketching', we consider a **sketch** to be something that a designer creates as part of their own private process. They may share it with other designers, but it is not intended for discussion or evaluation with users.

PURPOSE OF PROTOTYPING

The purpose of prototyping is to generate successive design solutions which can be evaluated with users so that the team learns more about the problem or its solution, and moves towards delivering a useful and usable system. As we saw in Chapters 3 and 6, user-centred design is a cyclical activity that involves continual experimentation. Almost all of the 'design solutions' that we use for these experiments are prototypes of varying kinds. Prototyping is an essential part of the process. For prototyping to be successful, the key point is to articulate clearly the learning objectives of every prototype: what are we planning to learn, and how?

Not only do we create potentially different kinds of prototype at different stages of a project, but we should also try at each stage to create alternative prototypes, so that

117

they can be compared with each other. By comparing the alternatives, we will usually come up with better ideas.

Always make more than one

One of the most tempting mistakes, in any field of design, is to seize upon the first solution that seems like a good one, and stop looking for others at that point. As you proceed down that path, you soon start to become attached to the idea and lose the ability to see the comparative benefits of alternative approaches, or even to recall the drawbacks that were obvious to you when the idea first came to you. Always try to come up with several different ideas at every stage, and carefully compare their relative strengths and weaknesses before you get too attached to one of them.

CHOOSING THE RIGHT SORT OF PROTOTYPE

There is a natural progression in the kind of prototypes produced during the life of a project. Early efforts will be more orientated towards testing out rough ideas. Later prototypes will focus more on details.

Evolutionary and throwaway prototypes

An evolutionary prototype is one where the same software code base is gradually expanded and improved to take in more and more functionality. Contrast this with a throwaway prototype, which is coded as a one-off task specifically in order to carry out a particular experiment, and is then discarded.

The evolutionary approach is often emphasised on Agile projects, either for the sake of speed, or from a belief that evolutionary prototyping is the correct method to use for incremental delivery. However, an incremental approach to delivering business value is not incompatible with throwaway prototyping. Throwaway prototypes can often be built efficiently, making use of existing code where possible, and can allow better focus on the problem being investigated and a wider range of design hypotheses. Besides, as discussed below, prototypes do not necessarily have to involve any coding at all.

Horizontal and vertical prototypes

A *horizontal* prototype is useful for exploring how well our product might support users in achieving all their goals. It focuses on showing the user the full range of functionality, usually without providing much interactivity at a detailed level.

Conversely, a *vertical* prototype allows the designers to test out detailed ideas for how the product will support users in carrying out a narrow range of tasks or achieving one specific goal.

Interactivity

An interactive prototype can be built using the product's target technology, or with a special-purpose prototyping tool. Interactive prototypes do not necessarily have to be electronic, as we will see below. Interactive models allow us to test sequences of pages and complex interactions in a way that is impossible with static mockups. However, not only does an interactive prototype take longer to create, but it focuses attention onto the dynamic behaviour of the interface and away from general consideration of the product scope. A good approach is to start prototyping as early as possible, and keep prototypes as low-tech as they can be for as long as possible.

Paper prototypes

Paper prototyping is the user experience specialist's secret weapon. It is an under-used technique that allows the design team to try out ideas from a very early stage of the project. User research should always come first, but as soon as the team has some understanding of the users, their environment and their goals, then paper prototypes can be produced to explore functionality with users.

A paper prototype can be created using large sheets of paper, such as A3. You can draw page elements using felt-tip pens. These can be drawn directly onto the main sheet of paper, or you can take a more modular approach, building up parts of the interface from smaller pieces of paper and sticky notes, which allows you to model interactivity by moving and replacing parts of the interface. Build the prototype so that a user can interact with it in an appropriate way. For example, interaction with a mouse and keyboard-based GUI can be simulated by having the test participant tap with their finger to represent a mouse click, or write on a sticky note, transparent paper or acetate to represent typing.

To run a test with a paper prototype, you will ideally have three people as well as the user themselves:

- The test moderator, who talks the user through the test.
- The 'computer', who moves the pieces of paper around in response to the actions the user takes.
- The scribe, who records observations. If each of these is written on a sticky note, then the findings can be taken straight into an affinity diagramming session after the testing has taken place.

Even though it is possible for one person to play two or even all three roles, this will almost always slow down the session and make it harder to maintain the test participant's interest.

Fidelity

Fidelity refers to the degree to which the appearance of the prototype matches the proposed appearance of the finished product. A **high-fidelity prototype** appears very similar to the final system; a **low-fidelity prototype** has some characteristics of the target system but is otherwise simple, usually in order to produce the prototype and test broad concepts quickly.

If it is to be interactive, a high-fidelity prototype is generally produced using the product's target technology. High-fidelity non-interactive mockups are often produced using graphics or photo editing software. High-fidelity prototypes are usually produced towards the later stages of a project, although there can be good reasons for producing them earlier; for example, if aesthetic and hedonic (pleasure-related) aspects of the user experience play a very important part in the product's value to the user. Usually, however, a focus on the details of visual design should be left as late as possible and it is a mistake to waste time on it too early (Figure 10.1).

Figure 10.1 High fidelity prototype

A preference for low-fidelity techniques is becoming more widely accepted as a fruitful way of learning about a product by getting quick feedback. We saw in Chapter 5 how 'quick and dirty' approaches to journey mapping and persona description are more generative than highly finished documentation. This is even truer when prototyping the user interface itself. When a prototype has an unfinished appearance, users and other stakeholders intuitively understand that they are participating in its ongoing design and refinement. This psychological effect is immensely helpful, and is exploited by electronic tools such as Balsamiq, which deliberately draw mockups so that they look as if they have been drawn by hand (Figure 10.2).

Figure 10.2 Mockup created in Balsamiq

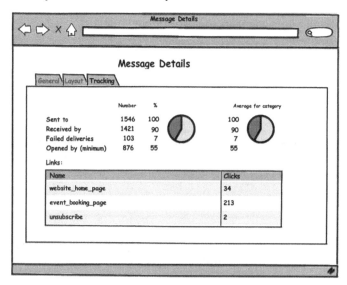

Wireframes

A standard technique for mapping out the structure of a user interface display is the **wireframe**. This is a stylised low-fidelity drawing of the display that shows all the logical elements but without any distracting features of visual design such as colour, fonts or images. Images are replaced by boxes of the right dimensions but containing only two diagonal lines. Meaningless text ('lorem ipsum' or *greeking*) is substituted for any paragraphs of meaningful text that could distract attention from the structure. Wireframes are traditionally done with a focus on layout, and have precisely correct proportions, but their value is largely in the way they help users and the project team to think about what is on each page and how it can support the user in carrying out their tasks by forming part of a coherent and consistent user journey. The term 'wireframe' is increasingly being used to refer to practically any mockup.

SUMMARY

A prototype is any kind of partial representation of a solution that can be used for evaluation with users. We can contrast this with a sketch, which is a vehicle for, and by-product of, visual thinking. A prototype should be associated with a learning objective. The more alternative prototypes are generated, the better the result is likely to be.

Evolutionary prototypes build on work already done, whereas throwaway prototypes are one-off products. Throwaway prototypes allow the team to explore a wider range of ideas. Vertical prototypes focus on a specific task or set of tasks in depth, whereas horizontal prototypes provide a broader view of the system in context.

Mockups, paper prototypes and other low-fidelity prototypes do not attempt to mimic details of the final product and are the most useful approaches in a project's early stages. Interactive and high-fidelity prototypes can be used later to explore details that are hard to replicate with low-fidelity approaches.

REFERENCES

ISO 9241-210:2019 (2019) *Ergonomics of Human-System Interaction – Part 210: Human-Centred Design for Interactive Systems*. International Organization for Standardization (ISO), Geneva.

Jacobs, H. (1965) *Frank Lloyd Wright: America's Greatest Architect*. Harcourt, Brace & World, New York.

FURTHER READING

Buley, L. (2013) *The User Experience Team of One*. Rosenfeld Media, Brooklyn, NY.

Buxton, B. (2007) *Sketching User Experiences: Getting the Design Right and the Right Design*. Morgan Kaufmann, San Francisco, CA.

Greenberg, S., Carpendale, S., Marquardt, N. and Buxton, B. (2011) *Sketching User Experiences: The Workbook*. Elsevier, Waltham, MA.

Snyder, C. (2003) *Paper Prototyping: The Fast and Easy Way to Design and Refine User Interfaces*. Morgan Kaufmann, San Francisco, CA.

EXAMPLE EXAMINATION QUESTIONS

1. **What are the benefits of low-fidelity prototypes?**

   1. They can be used to design user interface animations
   2. They encourage the design team to explore alternative designs
   3. They can be tested and refined quickly
   4. They can be used to assess technical feasibility before any code is written
   5. They can be developed by non-programmers
       a. 2, 3 and 4 only
       b. 2, 3 and 5 only
       c. 1, 2 and 5 only
       d. 1, 4 and 5 only

2. **You are in the early stages of the design of an in-car entertainment system that will allow passengers to download and view movies. What would be your first step?**

   a. Encourage the design team to think of various potential solutions to prevent them from becoming fixated on one design idea
   b. Explore the technical feasibility of using multi-touch, speech and head-up displays within an in-car environment
   c. Visit potential users to understand their current needs for such a system
   d. Create a paper prototype of a potential user interface and test it with users

3. **You are at the early design stage of a new system that will make significant changes to the way users carry out their work. The design team would like feedback on three alternative design ideas. Which user research technique would be MOST suitable?**

   a. Carry out a structured interview with existing users
   b. Carry out a usability test with a high-fidelity prototype
   c. Run an online survey with existing users
   d. Carry out a usability test with a low-fidelity prototype

4. **A researcher asks a participant to carry out tasks with a hand drawn interface, where the participant uses his finger as a mouse. What technique is the researcher using?**

   a.   Paper prototyping

   b.   Sketching

   c.   Retrospective protocol analysis

   d.   Design studio

ANSWERS TO EXAMPLE QUESTIONS

1. The correct answer is (b).

Choice (1) is wrong because realistic animations are impossible to replicate with a paper prototype. Choice (4) is wrong because paper prototypes cannot assess technical feasibility. It is only option (b) that has the other choices, excluding (1) and (4).

2. The correct answer is (c).

The purpose of this question is to make sure candidates realise that the first step in a project is not to prototype or think of design solutions at all, but to speak with users without any preconceptions about how the design might look. This makes (c) the best answer. (a) and (d) are sensible steps to take once the design process has begun, but neither should be the first step. Similarly, (b) will be important once the user's need for the service has been established, but there is no point exploring the technical feasibility until the users' needs have been uncovered.

3. The correct answer is (d).

(a) and (c) are wrong because they will collect opinion data: this will almost certainly be overwhelmingly negative because users are being asked to work differently. An additional problem with (a) is that the interviews will be 'structured', which omits the possibility of discovering findings outside the team's current way of thinking. What's needed here is some indication of the problems (if any) that people will have with the new approach, so some kind of behavioural observations are called for. This leaves (b) and (d) as the possible choices. Since we are at the early stages of design, and since the design team have three alternative designs, a test of a low-fidelity prototype would make more sense than a test with a high-fidelity prototype because the prototypes can be created more quickly. The low-fidelity prototype has the additional advantage that the systems will not look too 'finished', which means users are more likely to see the designs as early concepts and not finished designs.

4. The correct answer is (a).

(b) is wrong because sketching is the process of generating ideas and sketches are rarely suitable for paper prototyping. (c) is wrong because this technique requires the participants to view a video of themselves using the system and narrate what they were doing. (d) is wrong because a design studio is a collaborative sketching activity attended by designers. This leaves (a) as the correct answer.

11 USABILITY EVALUATION

> The proof of the pudding is in the eating.
>
> Old English saying

INTRODUCTION

This chapter describes how to assess the usability of a product, service or system. There are two ways of evaluating the usability of a system: **usability inspection** and *usability testing*. While usability testing involves having users work with the product or prototype and attempt to carry out tasks, usability inspection can be carried out by one or more individuals within the design team, without needing to involve any test participants.

We start by looking at ways in which a single person can inspect a system and draw conclusions about its usability. In particular, we consider guidelines such as Jakob Nielsen's (1993) *usability heuristics*. We move on to a discussion of how to conduct moderated usability tests, and stress the importance of these as the only reliable indicator of usability. We look at how to prioritise and report on usability test findings, before finally thinking about how to evaluate the accessibility of systems.

LEARNING OBJECTIVES

After reading this chapter you will be able to:

Remember	• Recall Nielsen's usability heuristics and have an awareness of other usability principles
	• State the different kinds of usability evaluation
	• Record the data from usability evaluations
	• State the difference between a usability inspection and a usability test
	• State the difference between observation and interpretation
	• Identify W3C's (2018) Web Content Accessibility Guidelines as an important standard in the field of web accessibility
Apply	• Plan usability evaluations to test design hypotheses
	• Interpret the data from usability tests to distinguish high and low severity usability problems
	• Moderate a usability test
	• Choose between good and poor tasks for a usability test

USABILITY INSPECTION

A well-known form of usability inspection is *heuristic evaluation* (Nielsen, 1993). This is based on systematically examining the user interface with a view to assessing its compliance with generally applicable principles (heuristics) of usable design.

Many usability researchers have proposed lists of guidelines that can be used in a heuristic evaluation. For example, Ben Shneiderman et al. (2016) define eight 'golden rules' of user interface design; Susan Weinschenk and Dean Barker (2000) provide a list that has been adapted to be suitable for speech interfaces. However, by far the most widely referenced is Jakob Nielsen's (1993) list of 10 usability heuristics.

Nielsen's usability heuristics

1. Visibility of system status
2. Match between system and the real world
3. User control and freedom
4. Consistency and standards
5. Help users recognise, diagnose and recover from errors
6. Error prevention
7. Recognition rather than recall
8. Flexibility and efficiency of use
9. Aesthetic and minimalist design
10. Help and documentation

Let's look at these heuristics.

1. Visibility of system status

The user should be able to understand what the system is doing at any time. Has it accepted their input? Is it processing it? If so, how long will it take? Is it waiting for more input? These considerations apply at many levels. Buttons should provide visual feedback showing both that they will be activated if the user clicks or taps, and that they have been activated when they do.

A wizard or other sequence of screens should provide information about the current position of the transaction. When the user starts a new session using the application, it should provide information showing that it remembers the user's previous work, together with their preferences and settings.

2. Match between system and the real world

The language used in the interface should match the language that comes naturally to the user when talking and thinking about the subject domain. The concepts used, and the relationships between them, should make sense to the user.

3. User control and freedom

The user should be free to take whatever action they want at any point. The system should be able to remember what the user is doing so that they can resume a task later if they need to take a break for any reason.

4. Consistency and standards

When people talk about an interface being 'intuitive', what they really mean is that it should be familiar. This means taking into account all the user's previous experience with interfaces, as discussed in Chapter 8. The producers of major operating systems, such as Apple, Google and Microsoft, publish style guides defining how interfaces should work on their platform – these should be followed.

5. Help users recognise, diagnose and recover from errors

This guideline covers both error conditions that have arisen in the software, and mistakes that users themselves have made.

6. Error prevention

Even better than helping users to recover from errors is making it impossible for them to make mistakes in the first place. Choosing the right user interface controls will help with this. Wherever possible, the interface should constrain the user's input so as to make it impossible to enter data of an invalid type. The next step is to help the user to enter data that is not only valid, but actually correct. We can see an example of this in the way that websites ask the user for their postal address. The most basic way of doing this would be to provide text input fields, such as 'Address Line 1', 'Address Line 2', 'Town' and 'Postcode', and leave it to the user to fill them in correctly. It is better to ask for the user's postcode, check it against a list of valid postcodes, and then ask them to choose from a list of the actual addresses at that postcode. A similar approach can be taken if asking for details of the user's car – the registration number can be checked against an online database that will then provide the details without the user needing to enter them.

7. Recognition rather than recall

It is extremely hard for human beings to recall random strings of letters and numbers unaided – yet some systems designers still persist in expecting them to, for example by enforcing the use of passwords that not only must adhere to complex rules about the use of special characters, numbers, capital letters and so on, but also must be changed frequently. We are far better at recognising words and phrases when they are presented to us as choices in a list; we are even better at recognising pictures, especially pictures of people's faces.

8. Flexibility and efficiency of use

It almost goes without saying that it should be possible to carry out tasks with the minimum expenditure of time and effort.

9. Aesthetic and minimalist design

The important word in this guideline is 'minimalist'. Nothing should appear in the interface unless there is a reason for it: preferably a reason that directly supports the achievement of the user's goals.

10. Help and documentation

Help and documentation should be available, appropriate and usable. They should be structured around the real tasks that users need to carry out, and the problems that they are likely to encounter, as discovered during user research and usability testing. The aim should be to design an interface that is so easy to use that no help or documentation is required – but this is not an excuse for not producing any.

Usability heuristics in service design

Usability guidelines such as Nielsen's heuristics originated as tools for assessing the user interface of software applications. However, they provide a sound basis for evaluating more complex socio-technical systems. For example, consider a service designed to enable citizens to file their tax returns, whether online or by any other means. We might ask questions such as:

- Can the user find out whether their tax return has been received? Can they find out whether it has been approved or not? (Heuristic 1)

- Are communications with the user couched in terms that they can understand and which relate to everyday life, or are they rooted in arcane taxation-related terminology? (Heuristic 2)

- Is information on previous returns available? (Heuristics 1 and 7)

- Is simple and effective guidance given to minimise the risk of errors? (Heuristics 6 and 10)

USABILITY TESTING

With usability inspection, a usability specialist can find any glaring defects that may be present in the usability of an interface. This is a form of negative testing. Finding errors does not provide confidence that users will be able to achieve their goals effectively, efficiently and with satisfaction. For that we need to employ usability testing.

There is only one way to know if a system is usable

A product or system is usable if, and only if, the specified users can achieve their specified goals with effectiveness, efficiency and satisfaction in the specified context of use.

You can find usability problems by inspecting the product or by testing its intrinsic properties, but you cannot prove its usability that way. You must find out if real users can use it to achieve realistic goals.

Usability testing can and should be carried out throughout the user-centred design cycle. It is the most effective tool at our disposal for ensuring that the system meets the users' needs. It involves a user attempting to carry out tasks with guidance and observation from a specialist – the test *moderator* – while thinking aloud. This means that the test participant provides a running commentary on what is going through their head when trying to use the interface.

Types of test

Usability tests are either **formative** or **summative**. A formative test is one whose output is used to feed back into the design of the product. Most usability testing falls into this category. By contrast, a summative test evaluates the usability of a product in order to see whether it meets predefined criteria, for example as part of a formal release procedure, quality audit or procurement exercise.

In-person usability tests involve the moderator and participant being physically present in the same place. These can sometimes be run in the participant's own environment, but normally there are several participants to get through in one day, which rules this out. In these cases you will want to run the tests at your own premises or at some other location that is easily accessible for the participants. A high-end approach would be to use a special-purpose usability testing lab equipped with commonly used phones, tablets and computers, a two-way mirror that allows observers to watch the session without being seen, recording equipment and eye-tracking kit.

It is increasing normal to run *remote* usability tests over the internet. This is much cheaper than running in-person tests. There are now many special-purpose software tools that support the process and record the test, but any screen-sharing software with a recording function can be used. Remote usability tests provide the moderator with reduced ability to interact with the participant and observe their reactions. This must be balanced against the low cost and comparative administrative ease of remote testing.

An extreme version of the remote usability test is the **unmoderated usability test**. Here, the participant uses the instructions they have been given to carry out the activities in their own time. They record the session for the researcher's review later on. Clearly, this type of test provides the lowest possible degree of opportunity for the researcher to interact with the participant and gain insight into their reactions. Perhaps the greatest risk is that the participant will fail to 'think aloud' sufficiently, reducing the overall usefulness of the test. If the budget is tight, unmoderated tests can be useful when testing small, well-defined pieces of design.

Steps involved in running a test

Executing a usability test involves the following steps:

1. Identify research questions that need to be answered
2. Identify and recruit some test participants
3. Devise test tasks and scenarios that will answer the questions
4. Prepare the environment for running the test
5. Moderate the test
6. Record your findings
7. Prioritise the issues

Identifying research questions

The types of questions that need to be answered will change and develop over the course of a project. Initially, you will want to know general things like:

- Do the concepts embodied in this design match the users' mental model?
- Does the interface support a sequence of tasks that is realistic for the user?
- Will the system as envisaged genuinely be useful?

Time invested on getting real experimental data to answer these questions at an early stage is time very well spent. Later, you will want to answer more specific questions such as:

- How long does it take the user to understand how to carry out a task?
- Does the user 'get it right first time'?
- For specific elements of form labelling, microcontent and navigation: does the user notice them? Do they understand them?
- How long does it take the user to complete the task?
- Does the user report any impatience, confusion or dissatisfaction?

At some points you may also want to compare alternative design options to see which work best.

As far as possible, the research questions should frame the issues in terms of the user's ability to carry out tasks, rather than focusing on details of the interface.

Recruiting test participants

The research questions will be based on the specific user groups or personas for whom the task is relevant. For our usability testing we need to recruit suitable representatives of those groups. We saw in Chapter 4 what makes someone a suitable representative.

Recruiting test participants and managing all the associated administration is a time-consuming task. There are agencies who will look after the recruitment and management of participants for both face-to-face and remote usability testing. Alternatively you may be able to recruit participants directly from your customer base. Either way, it is important to develop a *screener*. This is a questionnaire which can be used to confirm that an individual is indeed a good match for the 'specified user' in ISO 9241-11 (2018) terms.

To ensure that participants keep the appointment and take the session seriously, it is a good idea to offer them something in exchange for taking part. This could take the form of money, vouchers for ecommerce sites or similar. If the participants are your customers, you may be able to offer them something of value as part of that relationship, such as early access to products or discounts.

How many test participants are required? This is a controversial topic. The more participants, the better; then again, even one participant is very much better than none. When running formative tests in an iterative process, it is more valuable to test frequently than to involve a large number of participants each time. Around five participants may be enough to derive useful results from each prototype. As this is not a statistically significant sample size, it will not allow you to make numerical or statistical comparisons, but it will let you get a feel for the answers to questions like the ones mentioned above.

Some teams have a regular usability testing schedule where they book participants and facilities on a regular basis at the same time every week, rather than only starting to organise a test session when they have something specific to test. Summative testing will involve many more participants, carefully chosen to give more thorough representation of the expected user population.

Devising test tasks and scenarios

We saw in Chapter 5 how we can distil our user research findings into key tasks and user stories. These give us a concise record of what user goals, tasks and activities must be supported by the system, and which are the most important. We can produce prototypes, as described in Chapter 10, representing possible designs for supporting those tasks, and explore their usefulness with usability testing. The general procedure for usability testing is the same regardless of the prototype's degree of fidelity.

The key point to remember when designing test tasks is that they should be oriented towards real user goals. The test participant should be given tasks that are meaningful to them, and represent things they really would want to get done with the system. They should be challenged to carry out the tasks with a minimum of direction from the moderator.

The tasks to be tested should be written down in advance. This will help to ensure that each participant is given the same tasks. Each task should have success criteria defined. What does it mean to say that the task was carried out successfully? This might include multiple measures of effectiveness and efficiency.

The moderator needs to set the scene and provide meaningful, realistic detail that will create the appropriate context for the participant. The test scenario is the story that we tell the participant so that they can imagine themselves in the situation described and recognise the task as something they would typically want to do.

Preparing the environment

If the participants are coming to you, you will need to have facilities for welcoming them, a place where they can wait until they are needed and refreshments. A printed form for the participant to record their informed consent should be available. The moderator also needs to have the scenario description ready. This might contain a detailed word-by-word script. Any important aspects of the technical environment should be checked in advance – for example, if an internet connection is required, then it must be available.

Preparation must be made for the session to be video recorded. The recording should preferably focus on the user interface and show how the user is interacting with it. Additionally, it is sometimes helpful to have a parallel recoding of the user's facial expressions. If used, eye tracking (see Chapter 9) is normally done separately as a special kind of test.

Moderating a test

As the test moderator, your job is to ensure that you gain the greatest possible amount of valid, relevant information that will allow the research questions to be answered. This can be done by following the steps summarised in Figure 11.1 and listed below.

Figure 11.1 Key steps in conducting a usability test

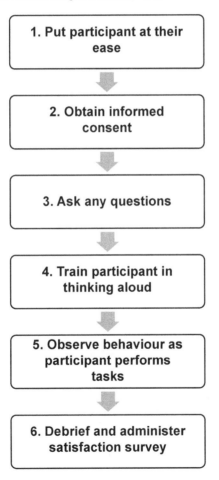

1. Put participant at their ease

2. Obtain informed consent

3. Ask any questions

4. Train participant in thinking aloud

5. Observe behaviour as participant performs tasks

6. Debrief and administer satisfaction survey

1. Put the participant at their ease. Welcome them and ensure that they are comfortable. Explain to them the purpose of the test and your respective roles. Make sure that they understand it is the product that is being tested, not them. Make it clear that you want full and honest feedback on the product being tested. It can be helpful to stress that you were not involved in creating it – if the participant believes that is the case, they may try to avoid offending you with negative feedback.

2. Obtain the participant's informed consent (see Chapter 4).

3. Ask any questions that you need answers to regarding the participant and their context.

4. Explain how think-aloud testing works. The participant needs to tell you at every stage what they are trying to do, what they are looking for or expecting to find presented in the interface, and what decisions they make as they go through the process. They must tell you whenever they are confused by something or get stuck. Explain that you would like them to ask you any questions that occur to them, but warn them that they may get a non-committal answer or none at all. This is not due to rudeness but to your need to see what would happen if they were using the interface alone, without any guidance.

   It is helpful to give a quick demonstration yourself of how thinking aloud is done. You might also ask the participant to do a practice run. In both cases, it is a good idea to choose a task that is as different as possible from the real ones that you are about to go through, so that the participant is not inappropriately 'primed' to say certain types of things.

5. Now for the main part of the test. Give the participant the tasks to do and observe what happens. When describing the tasks, it is important to use language that is easy to understand and does not give any clues regarding what the participant should look for in the interface. For example, if you are testing whether users will notice the 'unsubscribe' button on a web page, do not say 'Now see if you can work out how to unsubscribe yourself.' Say something like, 'Imagine that you've decided you wouldn't like to receive any more communications from this company – take some action to sort that out.'

   The most important thing for the moderator to do is nothing. In other words, you should not answer any questions or give any guidance on how to use the interface. If the participant asks you how to do something, use the boomerang technique – turn the question back to the participant. If they ask, 'What is this button for?', ask them 'What do you think it's for?' Do not allow the session to be diverted into any irrelevant discussions. If the participant says something that does not require an answer, then ignore it or make an encouraging noise. There is no need to praise them for anything that they manage to do.

   Some participants find that thinking aloud comes much more naturally to them than others. If they are not saying enough, ask **open questions**, completely free of reference to the interface details, such as 'What are you thinking'?

   If the participant gets completely stuck, then there may come a point at which they are clearly in such discomfort that you feel compelled either to help them complete the task or end the session. In this case, you may be able to move on to the next task in your plan and salvage some more benefit from the time you have both invested.

6. When all the tasks have been completed or the allotted time is over, you may want to administer a satisfaction survey such as a SUS survey (see Chapter 6). Also allow some time for answering questions and collecting any comments that the participant may want to make.

Recording usability issues

Defining the tasks clearly in advance, including the associated success criteria, makes it relatively straightforward to record the results of the usability test. You will also want to record your observations of things you noticed about what happened when the user tried to carry out the tasks. Make sure that you record what you saw and heard, rather than just your interpretation of what might be the reason for the observation. Interpretation is of course valuable, but must be kept separate, so that the observations can be accurately and objectively grouped, compared and analysed.

As discussed in Chapter 4, this can be done formally, by filling in a spreadsheet or other tabular record, or informally, by writing each observation on a sticky note. A formal approach is appropriate when carrying out a summative test; an informal approach will often work better for formative tests.

Prioritising usability issues

The objective of usability testing is often framed in terms of finding as many problems as possible. It is perhaps more accurate to say that the test should answer as many questions as possible, as conclusively as possible. Findings can be positive as well as negative.

Usability problems can be categorised according to three key criteria: *impact*, *frequency* and *persistence*. This allows us to create an action plan for dealing with them.

Issues with a high *impact* are typically those that affect the completion rate of tasks. The more severely the completion rate is affected, the higher the impact. We also need to take into account the importance of the task itself: it is especially important to address issues that affect critical tasks.

Frequency is a measure of how many test participants encountered the issue. It is quite common to find an issue that only affects one participant. If there are only four or five in the sample, it is difficult to know how important the issue is and a judgement must be made or further testing done. If an issue affects multiple participants it needs to be addressed.

The *persistence* of an issue is the degree to which it annoys and disrupts use of the system by recurring frequently. For example, if there is an issue that occurs on every page of a website, then user satisfaction is bound to be impacted.

One way of using these three measures is to group issues into four grades of priority: low, medium, serious and critical. If the issue scores highly on all three measures, then it is critical. If it scores highly on two, it is serious. If it scores highly on one, then it is medium; if it does not score highly on any, then it is low.

EVALUATING ACCESSIBILITY

The World Wide Web Consortium (W3C) is the standards body for web protocols. The Web Content Accessibility Guidelines (WCAG) published as part of W3C's Web Accessibility Initiative (WAI) give numerous recommendations for making web-based systems more accessible. The guidelines are specifically aimed at improving access for:

a wider range of people with disabilities, including accommodations for blindness and low vision, deafness and hearing loss, limited movement, speech disabilities, photosensitivity, and combinations of these, and some accommodation for learning disabilities and cognitive limitations (W3C, 2018)

But they make the key point that 'following these guidelines will also often make Web content more usable to users in general'. The guidelines are applicable to any system with an HTML-based user interface.

The WCAG-WAI guidelines are a valuable resource for the evaluation of accessibility. Testable success criteria are provided for each guideline. There are three levels of conformance, from A at the lowest level to AAA at the highest.

The general principles set out in the guidelines are that web content should be:

- **Perceivable**: the user must have access to the content and controls in a form that they can perceive.

- **Operable**: it must be possible for the user to operate the navigation and other controls with a device that they are able to use, such as the keyboard.

- **Understandable**: the user must be able to read or hear and interpret the text that is presented, and predict the way the system will respond to their actions.

- **Robust**: the content must be coded in such a way that it can be interpreted by a wide range of device software, including assistive technology.

SUMMARY

There are two main types of usability evaluation: usability inspection and usability testing. Inspection can be carried out by one individual using a set of guidelines such as Nielsen's usability heuristics, which are the best known among many sets of system usability principles.

A usability test evaluates empirically whether the specified user can carry out tasks effectively, efficiently and with satisfaction, using a prototype that has been created to embody one or more design hypotheses. The user is given realistic and meaningful tasks that relate to their own typical objectives in using the system. The test moderator must allow the participant to work completely unaided, and must record their observations – what they see and hear – without interpretation. Test results can be assigned a priority of critical, serious, medium or low, depending on how many of the following criteria they score highly on: impact, frequency and persistence.

W3C's (2018) Web Content Accessibility Guidelines (WCAG-WAI) are the most commonly referenced standard for web accessibility.

REFERENCES

ISO 9241-11:2018 (2018) *Ergonomics of Human-System Interaction – Part 11: Usability: Definitions and Concepts*. International Organization for Standardization (ISO), Geneva.

Nielsen, J. (1993) *Usability Engineering*. Morgan Kaufmann, San Diego, CA.

Shneiderman, B., Plaisant, C., Cohen, M., Jacobs, S., Elmqvist, N. and Diakopoulos, N. (2016) *Designing the User Interface: Strategies for Effective Human-Computer Interaction*. Pearson, Harlow.

W3C (2018) Web Content Accessibility Guidelines (WCAG) 2.1. W3C Recommendation 05 June 2018. Available from: https://www.w3.org/TR/WCAG21/

Weinschenk, S. and Barker, D.T. (2000) *Designing Effective Speech Interfaces (Vol. 1)*. Wiley, New York.

FURTHER READING

ISO/IEC 25066:2016(en) (2016) *Systems and Software Engineering – Systems and Software Quality Requirements and Evaluation (SQuaRE) – Common Industry Format (CIF) for Usability – Evaluation Report*. International Organization for Standardization (ISO), Geneva.

Krug, S. (2014) *Don't Make Me Think, Revisited: A Common Sense Approach to Web Usability*. New Riders, Berkeley, CA.

Rubin, J. and Chisnell, D. (2008) *Handbook of Usability Testing: How to Plan, Design and Conduct Effective Tests*. Wiley, Indianapolis, IN.

Tedesco, D. and Tranquada, F. (2013) *The Moderator's Survival Guide: Handling Common, Tricky, and Sticky Situations in User Research*. Morgan Kaufmann, Waltham, MA.

EXAMPLE EXAMINATION QUESTIONS

1. **Which of the following data sets could be useful for recording quantitative data during usability evaluations?**

   a. Success rate, error rates, observations about the pathways taken by users

   b. Task time, error rates, satisfaction questionnaire ratings

   c. Task time, observations about pathways taken by users, problems experienced

   d. Success rates, problems experienced, satisfaction questionnaire ratings

2. **You are evaluating a new interactive voice response system in which users are expected to make selections from a telephone keypad. Which one of the following research questions could be answered with a small number of participants (say five)?**

   a.   Are users quicker with the new system or with the old system?

   b.   How much would people pay to use the service?

   c.   What are the demographic characteristics of the target audience?

   d.   What are the main usability issues with the system?

3. **Which of the following are useful objectives from a usability test?**

   1.   Check the system is easy to use

   2.   Ensure users understand the terminology

   3.   Assess if the user experience is acceptable

   4.   Decide if one version of the interface is more usable than another version

   5.   See if users can export their saved files with the web version of the user interface

   6.   Discover usability issues with the user registration process

        a.   1, 2 and 4 only

        b.   3, 5 and 6 only

        c.   1 and 3 only

        d.   2, 5 and 6 only

4. **Place the following stages of a usability test in order.**

   1.   Recruit users

   2.   Agree the test objectives

   3.   Run a pilot test

   4.   Create task scenarios

        a.   1, 2, 3, 4

        b.   2, 1, 4, 3

        c.   1, 4, 2, 3

        d.   2, 3, 4, 1

5. **You are moderating a usability test. The participant has been working quickly through a test task but then pauses for a while. Which of the following would be suitable prompts?**

   1. What are you thinking right now?
   2. If you were the designer, how would you have designed this screen?
   3. Are you looking for the 'Help' function?
   4. Please remember to think out loud
   5. Let's stop this task here and come back to it later
   6. What do you want to see here?
      a. 1 and 4 only
      b. 2 and 6 only
      c. 1, 3, 5 and 6 only
      d. 2, 3, 4 and 5 only

6. **Which of the following tasks would be suitable to use in a usability test of a stylus-based tablet input device aimed at digital illustrators?**

   1. You have just received your new tablet device. Install the product and check that it works correctly
   2. Configure the tablet for left-handed use
   3. Open the software extension for the tablet and set the Mapping Mode to 'Pen'
   4. Adjust the feel of the eraser to the point where it feels hard
   5. Compare the responsiveness of the device when used over Bluetooth and when connected via USB
      a. 3, 4 and 5 only
      b. 1, 2 and 4 only
      c. 1 and 2 only
      d. 4 and 5 only

ANSWERS TO EXAMPLE QUESTIONS

1. The correct answer is (b).

All items are valid types of data that can be collected during usability tests, but option (b) is the only option that has just quantitative data types. The other options include mixtures of quantitative and qualitative data.

2. The correct answer is (d).

This question aims to test a candidate's understanding of the kinds of research that can be done with small sample sizes. (a) is incorrect because this question will require some kind of statistical comparison, and this isn't plausible with a small sample size. (b) is incorrect because this is an opinion-based question that again will need a large sample size. (c) is incorrect because a small sample size will badly skew the results. (For example, if four of the five participants are male, does this mean 80% of the population is male?) (d) is the correct answer as a well-run usability test will identify the main usability issues even if the sample size is relatively small.

3. The correct answer is (d).

(1) is a poor choice for a usability objective because it is unmeasurable in its current state: what does 'easy to use' mean in this context? (3) suffers from the same problem: what does 'acceptable' mean? Neither of these is specific enough to be a useful objective in a usability test. The remaining choices are specific enough, which makes (d) the correct choice.

4. The correct answer is (b).

(2) has to be the first choice because the test objectives will have implications for the users who are recruited and the task scenarios that are used. (4) must come before (3) because the pilot test cannot take place without the scenarios. The only answer with (2), (4) and (3) in order is choice (b). It's possible that user recruitment (1) could take place last, although it would be inefficient to do so (it makes more sense to start recruitment as early as possible since this can cause a delay).

5. The correct answer is (a).

This question tests if candidates realise their role as a test moderator is simply to help participants to keep talking and not to influence their stream of consciousness. (2) and (6) are poor questions because participants are not designers: it's not clear how the design team can take action on what the participant says here. (3) is a poor choice because it may bias the participant to look for help or to confabulate and say they were looking for help when they were not. (5) is a poor choice because the participant isn't struggling: the user has simply paused. This is when the researcher learns about the problems the participant is experiencing and this shouldn't be cut short. This leaves (1) and (4) that are both good prompts to make and so (a) the correct answer.

6. The correct answer is (b).

This question aims to test that candidates can choose between good and poor tasks in a usability test. (3) is a poor task because it explains to users how they should do the task (it is more like a user acceptance test task). (5) is a poor task because it is not realistic: this isn't the kind of task a user would normally expect to carry out. The remaining tasks are all tasks that real users would carry out with the product, which makes (b) the correct answer.

12 THE CONTEXT FOR UX (2)
Project Processes

Each refinement implies a number of design decisions based upon a set of design criteria ... Students must be taught to be conscious of the involved decisions and to critically examine and to reject solutions, sometimes even if they are correct as far as the result is concerned; they must learn to weigh the various aspects of design alternatives in the light of these criteria. In particular, they must be taught to revoke earlier decisions, and to back up, if necessary even to the top.

Niklaus Wirth (1971)

INTRODUCTION

This chapter covers some additional topics that are not part of the syllabus for the BCS Foundation Certificate in User Experience. This is background information that will prove helpful when using the core techniques in practice. It is largely concerned with how to reconcile the model of system design activity presented in the earlier chapters with other prevalent models.

First, we look at the Agile development approach. We then discuss design thinking and the double diamond model. In each case, we show how the model is basically consistent with the user-centred design cycle but requires some adjustments. We also consider how UX work fits in with the Agile delivery life cycle as promoted by the GOV.UK service manual.

Finally, we look at some approaches to systematising the preparatory work that needs to be done to get either user research or UX design work off the ground: style guides, design systems, ResearchOps and DesignOps.

The syllabus for the BCS Foundation Certificate in User Experience is covered in Chapters 3–11. The material in this chapter is supplementary and is not examinable.

UX AND AGILE DEVELOPMENT

The Agile approach to software development includes the following features:

- Multidisciplinary, ideally co-located teams.
- A strong emphasis on continual, face-to-face communication.
- Instead of formally documented requirements, a continually managed and prioritised *backlog* of user stories and an emphasis on prototyping.
- Iterative development organised into short (usually two-week) fixed periods, known as *iterations*, *sprints* or *timeboxes*.
- Frequent incremental delivery of software as early as possible.

The overall result of these measures, if done properly, is a dramatic reduction in the likelihood of delivering a product that is not fit for purpose. This is mainly because the iterative development approach allows for frequent feedback, ensuring that the project does not go too far off track in terms of delivering what users need. This is contrasted with the so-called *waterfall* approach, where an attempt is made to agree and document all the requirements before development is started – an approach with very little scope for feedback and hence learning.

In Scrum, the most well-known variety of Agile, there are three fixed roles: Development Team Member, Product Owner and Scrum Master. The Product Owner is the single individual who is responsible for managing and prioritising the backlog. In common with other well-known Agile methods, Scrum does not define the method to be used for finding out the users' needs or evaluating how well the product meets them at any stage.

Agile thinking is deeply ingrained in many software product development organisations. In one way, Agile and user-centred design complement each other beautifully: both are based on continuous iteration and prototyping, recognising the importance of validated learning and short feedback loops. However, in practice there can be tensions and difficulties that arise from the variations in approach between developers, analysts and designers.

The most popular Agile approach, Scrum, is often interpreted as enshrining the principle that a project should start delivering usable software from the end of the very first iteration. This can be a problem for user researchers, who want to carry out user research before creating any prototypes. Not only that, but if the development team rushes into building software before a coherent design concept has been created, the result is likely to be a product with an incoherent user interface and many usability problems.

Possible countermeasures for this are:

- Insert *design spikes* into the process, where design issues can be explored outside the constraints of the sprint schedule.

- Have the UX practitioners keep one or two steps ahead of the developers by working on the sprints that are due to be developed later. This compromises the Agile ideal of a multidisciplinary team working together to create solutions for the user stories in each sprint.

- Make a UX specialist the Product Owner.

- Be as well prepared as possible for the work on interaction design and visual design by putting in place a *design system* (see below).

- Have a *Sprint Zero* before development commences, where research can be done and a *style guide* created. However, this is unlikely to be sufficient.

- If the team uses a method like Dynamic Systems Development Method (DSDM), this includes a Foundations phase where research can be carried out; but what is really needed is a way of carrying out all UX research and design activities continually, throughout the project.

- Treat research, design and development as separate projects or sub-projects and create opportunities for them to inform each other as the work progresses.

Since one of the proven strengths of Agile is its insistence on multidisciplinary teams, arguably the most productive approach is to keep the whole team together in a single project but ensure that the objectives of each iteration are not defined in terms of getting functionality 'done', but rather with reference to the validated learning approach described in Chapter 6, in terms of creating understanding.

UCD AND DESIGN THINKING

Sprints in Scrum should not be confused with *design sprints.* A design sprint (Knapp et al., 2016) is a process defined at Google Ventures for exploring a situation, generating a problem statement and creating a prototype solution within one week. This is an example of *design thinking* (Brown, 2009), which aims to apply a design mindset to enterprise-level situations.

A well-known metaphor in design thinking is the Design Council's *Double Diamond* (Design Council, 2007). This shows the project process graphically in terms of two phases: an initial discovery phase of divergent thinking, which narrows down to a single point where the problem has been tightly defined; and a later phase of solution creation, where divergent thinking is again employed to develop a range of design concepts for solutions to the problem, before converging again for delivery. Figure 12.1 shows the double diamond with its four associated design activities: Discover, Define, Develop, Deliver.

Figure 12.1 The double diamond

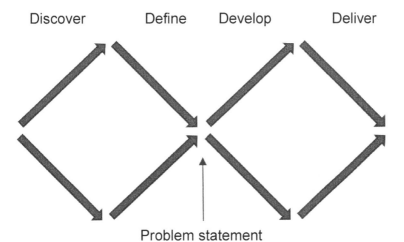

Discover   Define   Develop   Deliver

Problem statement

The four activities can clearly be related to the four main threads of the user-centred design helix (see Figure 3.2), although the fourth stage, 'Deliver', does not explicitly include evaluation with users. However, the double diamond itself shows the project as being divided into exactly two main parts, with the first being orientated towards producing a single definitive problem statement, and the second towards delivering a solution that satisfies the problem statement. Therefore the double diamond has been re-thought by many designers to show that consecutive phases of divergent and convergent thinking are indeed employed on design projects, but these phases are not necessarily restricted to two in number. On the contrary, arguably there should be one pair of diamonds for each iteration through the user-centred design cycle. In addition, the iterations do not have to form a linear sequence but can branch outwards to create a more complicated pattern reminiscent of the knitting on an Aran sweater (Figure 12.2).

Figure 12.2 The Aran sweater

UCD AND AGILE DELIVERY

The Agile delivery process promoted by the GOV.UK service manual includes the following phases for designing and developing a service:

- **Discovery**: this is very much a research-focused phase, so in terms of the UCD cycle, the main activity here is Understand the Context. This includes finding out about the users and their goals, as well as the wider technical and social environment that the solution must operate within, and the *policy intent* – arguably a very specific type of high-level stakeholder requirement. No prototype should be produced at this stage.

- **Alpha**: here, the team focuses on envisioning and building prototypes, evaluating them with users and developing a solid understanding of user needs. The prototypes should be aimed at testing the riskiest assumptions, as described in Chapter 6.

- **Beta**: this involves taking an iterative approach to develop the service into something that will meet the success measures defined in the Discovery phase. Key techniques here are hypothesis-driven experiments and usability testing. The Beta phase starts with a *private beta*, where a limited number of people are invited to participate in evaluating the service, and then moves into a *public beta*, where anyone who needs the service can use it

- **Live**: the team will become smaller at this point, but the service is still iteratively improved.

This structure fits in very well with the approach described in this book.

UX PROCESS MATURITY

Design systems, or *design languages*, developments from the older idea of *style guides*, are formats for re-using design work across teams and projects in an orderly way. These provide a consistent and coherent basis for design work and encompass, to varying degrees, elements of visual design and interaction design. Notable examples of design systems are:

- The BBC's Global Experience Language (GEL) (www.bbc.co.uk/gel/)

- The GOV.UK Design System (https://design-system.service.gov.uk/)

- Google's Material Design (https://material.io/)

- Microsoft's Fluent Design System (https://www.microsoft.com/design/fluent/)

- Apple's Human Interface Guidelines (https://developer.apple.com/design/human-interface-guidelines/)

The websites associated with each of these examples provide an excellent resource for anyone wanting to understand how interaction design and visual design outputs can be documented and organised at scale.

ResearchOps (https://medium.com/researchops-community) and *DesignOps* are two evangelising movements concerned with bringing order and scalability to user research and design respectively, as well as playing a role in balancing out the influence of Agile with other perspectives.

SUMMARY

The principles underlying Agile development are entirely in tune with user-centred design. However, Agile projects are often focused on delivering 'working software' at too early a stage, when delivering improved understanding would be a more appropriate objective.

The double diamond activities – Discover, Define, Develop, Deliver – are compatible with user-centred design, but a truly iterative approach contains multiple 'diamonds', not just two.

The GOV.UK Agile Delivery approach is an excellent example of how to use user-centred design for developing a service in practice, at scale and at pace.

The design systems and design languages defined by major software companies and others such as the UK Government and the BBC are useful examples of how to standardise interaction design and visual design.

REFERENCES

Brown, T. (2009) *Change By Design*. HarperCollins, New York.

Design Council (2007) *Eleven Lessons: Managing Design in Eleven Global Companies – Desk Research Report*. Design Council, London.

Knapp, J., Zeratsky, J. and Kowitz, B. (2016) *Sprint: How to Solve Big Problems and Test New Ideas in Just Five Days*. Simon and Schuster, New York.

Wirth, N. (1971) Program development by stepwise refinement. *Communications of the ACM*, 14(4), 221–227.

FURTHER READING

Battles, M., Black, M., Malouf, D., Whitehead, C. and Bernstein, G. (2019) *DesignOps Handbook*. Available from: https://www.designbetter.co/designops-handbook

Gothelf, J. and Seiden, J. (2013) *Lean UX: Applying Lean Principles to Improve User Experience*. O'Reilly Media, Sebastopol, CA.

Jones, J.C. (1992) *Design Methods*. Wiley, New York.

Merholz, P. and Skinner, K. (2016) *Org Design for Design Orgs*. O'Reilly, Sebastopol, CA.

Perri, M. (2018) *Escaping the Build Trap*. O'Reilly Media, Sebastopol, CA.

Ratcliffe, L. and McNeill, M. (2011) *Agile Experience Design: A Digital Designer's Guide to Agile, Lean, and Continuous*. New Riders, Berkeley, CA.

Unger, R. and Chandler, C. (2012) *A Project Guide to UX Design: For User Experience Designers in the Field or in the Making*. New Riders, Berkeley, CA.

APPENDIX

A1 THE BCS FOUNDATION CERTIFICATE IN USER EXPERIENCE

The examination for the BCS Foundation Certificate in User Experience is a closed-book multiple choice test, delivered either on paper or online (see https://www.bcs.org/get-qualified/certifications-for-professionals/user-experience-certifications/bcs-foundation-certificate-in-user-experience/). There are 40 questions to be completed in one hour. The pass mark is 26/40, that is, 65%. The examination is designed to be achievable with 18 hours of study.

The level of knowledge required for each area of the syllabus is defined according to the Skills Framework for the Information Age (SFIA) *K levels*, as described on the BCS website. The full set of SFIA levels is shown in Table A1.1.

Table A1.1 SFIA K levels

Level	Level of knowledge	Level of skill and responsibility (SFIA)
K7		Set strategy, inspire and mobilise
K6	Evaluate	Initiate and influence
K5	Synthesise	Ensure and advise
K4	Analyse	Enable
K3	Apply	Apply
K2	Understand	Assist
K1	Remember	Follow

You will recognise the terms 'Apply', 'Understand' and 'Remember' from the lists of Learning Objectives at the start of the chapters in this book. All the learning objectives in the syllabus are at one of these three levels.

The maximum level for each top-level area of the syllabus is either Understand or Apply. This and the weighting, that is, the target number of questions in the exam, for each area are shown in Table A1.2.

Table A1.2 The syllabus areas with their maximum K levels and weighting

Syllabus area	Chapter	Maximum K level	Target number of questions
1. Guiding principles	3	Understand	2
2. User research	4	Apply	4
3. Illustrating the context of use	5	Apply	6
4. Measuring usability	6	Apply	2
5. Information architecture	7	Apply	6
6. Interaction design	8	Apply	4
7. Visual design	9	Understand	4
8. User interface prototyping	10	Apply	4
9. Usability evaluation	11	Apply	8
Total			40

INDEX